STRENGTHENING SUPPORT FOR LABOR MIGRATION IN TAJIKISTAN

ASSESSMENT AND RECOMMENDATIONS

DECEMBER 2020

ASIAN DEVELOPMENT BANK

ADB

© 2020 Asian Development Bank
6 ADB Avenue, Mandaluyong City, 1550 Metro Manila, Philippines
Tel +63 2 8632 4444; Fax +63 2 8636 2444
www.adb.org

Some rights reserved. Published in 2020.

ISBN 978-92-9262-471-2 (print), 978-92-9262-472-9 (electronic)
Publication Stock No. TCS200362
DOI: http://dx.doi.org/10.22617/TCS200362

The views expressed in this publication are those of the authors and do not necessarily reflect the views and policies of the Asian Development Bank (ADB) or its Board of Governors or the governments they represent.

ADB does not guarantee the accuracy of the data included in this publication and accepts no responsibility for any consequence of their use. The mention of specific companies or products of manufacturers does not imply that they are endorsed or recommended by ADB in preference to others of a similar nature that are not mentioned.

By making any designation of or reference to a particular territory or geographic area, or by using the term "country" in this document, ADB does not intend to make any judgments as to the legal or other status of any territory or area.

Please contact pubsmarketing@adb.org if you have questions or comments with respect to content, or if you wish to obtain copyright permission for your intended use that does not fall within these terms, or for permission to use the ADB logo.

Corrigenda to ADB publications may be found at http://www.adb.org/publications/corrigenda.

Notes:
In this publication, "$" refers to United States dollars.
ADB recognizes "Kyrgyzstan" as the Kyrgyz Republic and "Russia" as the Russian Federation.

Cover design by Claudette Rodrigo.

Contents

Tables, Figures, and Boxes

Acknowledgments

This report presents an analysis of the major socioeconomic impacts of labor migration in Tajikistan, along with recommendations for policy planners and administrators. It introduces international best practices associated with international migration in other Asia and Pacific countries, which are also dependent on remittances from overseas migrants. It focuses on formal migration administered by the Ministry of Labour, Migration and Employment (MOLME) of the Republic of Tajikistan.

The analysis covers recent trends of migration and needed support, as well as policy options for future predeparture and post-return services. Tables with data on other relevant issues (such as job replacement of the returning migrants, family separation, and risks of migration) provide a comprehensive understanding of the current conditions of migrants and migrant families.

The study team from the Asian Development Bank (ADB) that developed this report worked on the ADB-funded Skills and Employability Enhancement Project in Tajikistan, led by Eiko Kanzaki Izawa. Team members were Takashi Yamano, Aiko Kikkawa Takenaka, and Nahreen Farjana. Ryotaro Hayashi and Lisa-Marie Josefin Kreibich provided peer reviews. Rie Hiraoka provided a review as well as technical input. Madeline Dizon and Laureen Felisienne Tapnio provided coordination and administrative support.

Special thanks to Daler Safarov, manager of Project Administration Group of the ADB-funded Strengthening Technical and Vocational Education and Training Project in Tajikistan. He provided valuable advice and coordination support. Assisting him in gathering data and information were project administration group staff and consultants: Firdavs Jumaev, Sangin Boboev, Abdulmajid Bobokhonov,

Ismatullo Ismatulloev, and Jamshed Kuddusov. Former First Deputy Head of Migration Service Moyonsho Mahmadbekov also provided insightful inputs into this study.

Werner Liepach
Director General
Central and West Asia Department (CWRD)

Rie Hiraoka
Director
Social Sector Division (CWSS), CWRD

Eiko Kanzaki Izawa
Team Leader
Unit Head, Project Administration, CWSS, CWRD

Aiko Kikkawa Takenaka
Economist, Economic Analysis and Operational Support Division (EREA), Economic Research and Regional Cooperation Department (ERCD)

Takashi Yamano
Senior Economist,
EREA, ERCD

Madeline S. Dizon
Project Analyst,
CWSS, CWRD

Laureen Felisienne M. Tapnio
Operations Assistant
CWSS, CWRD

Nahreen Farjana
Consultant

Abbreviations

ADB	Asian Development Bank
ALC	adult learning center
BMET	Bureau of Manpower, Employment and Training (Bangladesh)
BNP2TKI	National Board for the Placement and Protection of Indonesian Overseas Workers (Indonesia)
BP3TKI	Agency for the Service, Placement and Protection of Indonesian Overseas Workers (Indonesia)
CIS	Commonwealth of Independent States
COVID-19	coronavirus disease
CSCG	Civil Society Contact Group
CSO	civil society organization
EUI	European University Institute
FAO	Food and Agricultural Organization
FEPB	Foreign Employment Promotion Board (Nepal)
FGD	focus group discussions
FMDW	female migrant domestic worker
G2G	government to government
GBAO	Gorno-Badakhshan Autonomous Oblast
GDP	gross domestic product
HRC	Human Rights Center
ILO	International Labour Organization
IMF	International Monetary Fund
IOM	International Organization for Migration
JICA	Japan International Cooperation Agency
KNOMAD	Global Knowledge Partnership on Migration and Development
MOLME	Ministry of Labour, Migration and Employment of Population of the Republic of Tajikistan
MOU	memorandum of understanding
MPI	Migration Policy Institute
MRITP	Market-Responsive Inclusive Training Program
NDS 2030	National Development Strategy of the Republic of Tajikistan for the period up to 2030
NGO	nongovernmental organization
OECD	Organisation for Economic Co-operation and Development
OSCE	Organization for Security and Co-operation in Europe
OWWA	Overseas Workers Welfare Administration (the Philippines)
PAG	project administration group
PDO	predeparture orientation
PDOS	predeparture orientation seminar
PEOS	preemployment orientation seminar
POEA	Philippine Overseas Employment Administration (the Philippines)
SDC	Swiss Agency for Development and Cooperation
SEEP	Skills and Employability Enhancement Project (Tajikistan)

SLBFE	Sri Lanka Bureau of Foreign Employment
TA	technical assistance
TOT	training of trainers
TRTA	transaction technical assistance
TVET	technical and vocational education and training
UN	United Nations
UNDP	United Nations Development Programme
UNHCR	United Nations High Commissioner for Refugees
WHO	World Health Organization

Executive Summary

Over the last decade, Tajikistan has steadily reduced poverty. International migration, an alternative livelihood option, has been a major driver of this economic advancement. Migration eases the pressure of unemployment and contributes to the foreign currency reserve. In 2019, Tajikistan received $2.7 billion as remittance, equivalent to 33.4% of gross domestic product (GDP).

Despite its economic opportunity for citizens, migration presents the government with challenges. The government must manage the outflow of migrant workers while ensuring their safety, rights, and welfare. To support the government's effort to strengthen its existing services, this report reviews the state of international migration, identifies effective practices to support international migrants in Asia, and provides recommendations to strengthen existing predeparture and post-arrival governmental services to Tajik migrants. Although the report was initiated before the coronavirus disease (COVID-19) outbreak, it touches on some issues relevant to dealing with the current pandemic.

The Tajik economy is not creating enough jobs for its rapidly growing labor force. Every year about half a million Tajiks leave the country for overseas employment, the majority of them male (85.5% in 2019) and short-term seasonal migrants (75%). Migrants are primarily from rural areas (85%) and young (85% between 15 and 44). The Russian Federation is the major destination country for Tajik migrants (97.6% in 2019). Longstanding ties from the Soviet era, language commonalities, migrant networks, significant wage differentials, as well as visa-free and on-arrival visa options make the Russian Federation a popular choice. A majority of migrant men work in the construction sector mainly as unskilled laborers, while migrant women are in the service sector. Although most migrants leave Tajikistan legally, some of them become irregular for various reasons, ranging from minor administrative to serious offenses (in December 2019, the number of migrants in the reentry ban list of the Russian Federation was 267,324). The International Organization for Migration defines irregular migration as the movement of persons that takes place outside the laws, regulations, or international agreements governing the entry into or exit from the state of origin, transit, or destination.

This report reveals major problems during the premigration state including lack of access to information and skills training opportunities and the high cost of migration—the highest passport cost among Commonwealth of Independent States (CIS) countries—and loans to pay for migration cost and maintaining family. Most migrant workers (85.5%) had no skills training before departing. A majority (86%) also relied on friends and relatives when applying for employment. Furthermore, nearly all migrants depended on informal networks for predeparture information and overseas employment.

Some challenges faced by Tajik migrants in the Russian Federation include unemployment for a month or more; difficulty in obtaining work permit and work patent from various government agencies in the Russian Federation; shortage of Ministry of Labor, Migration and Employment (MOLME) representatives to aid migrants; and limited access to legal remedies in the Russian Federation. Destination-country work and living situations pose another set of problems. The majority of migrants, low skilled and economically desperate, are willing to accept any working conditions. Most migrants also have nearly zero legal literacy. These conditions can lead to labor exploitation by employers and police abuse and extortion by criminal gangs. In addition, xenophobic attitudes in the Russian Federation, cited in interviews of returned migrants, are a major difficulty of working there. A majority of the migrants live and work in very poor and harsh conditions and reside in overcrowded apartments primarily to save money, resulting in poor hygiene and health. Furthermore, lack of knowledge regarding health, including sexual and reproductive health, has been identified among the migrants. Social and psychological adaptation of Tajik migrants is also difficult as most of them come from rural areas.

Challenges for returning migrants include difficulties in economic, social, and psychological reintegration. Migrant families use an overwhelming portion of remittances (94%) for private consumption, which is the most important component of GDP. However, remittances are rarely used for investments or to save for future contingencies, leaving migrants continually dependent on overseas employment for livelihood.

As a group, the migrants in the reentry ban list of the Russian Federation need support in removing their names from the list, assistance in finding alternative employment in the country or a different destination, and psychosocial counseling after return. Migrant families left behind are affected as well. Since a majority of the migrants are male, it adds further stress on women, adding economic activities to their traditional roles. Another issue of concern is the abandonment of spouses; various studies estimate that about 30% of the wives left behind by their husbands have been abandoned.

A majority of the migrants leave for overseas employment without any detailed knowledge of their destination country—relying almost entirely on information from informal sources such as family and friends. Migrant workers and other stakeholders identified the need for training and information related to language and skills training recognized in destination countries; remittance management; history, culture, rights, law, and documentation processes of destination countries; and support in the destination country including legal aid if needed. Other areas of concern noted are the need for job creation after

return as well as recognition of skills acquired in the destination country.

To provide migrant services, MOLME has established four predeparture centers under Migration Services. However, the staff are inadequately equipped with any structured training or materials on all issues pertaining to migration, including how to train and interact with migrants. In practice, they are busy dealing with migrants in the reentry ban list of the Russian Federation, instead of helping departing migrants. Additionally, the current digital information dissemination needs to be enhanced. During the current pandemic, digital information would assist migrants in finding information and services.

The economic crisis brought on by the COVID-19 pandemic has halted international migration flows, and remittances have decreased significantly. Strategies are needed to safeguard the livelihood of migrants, regardless of their migration and legal status, for returned migrants and stranded or working migrants in destination countries and their families. The government needs to work in close cooperation with destination-country governments and other development partners to devise tactics of safe migration options during and after the pandemic and ensure the continued inflow of remittances that are vital in meeting the daily needs of the recipient families.

To strengthen the existing migrant services of the government, this report briefly reviews migration structure and good practices in predeparture and post-return services conducted by selected labor-origin countries in Asia, with a focus on predeparture orientation (PDO). It recommends that predeparture and post-return service be catered to potential migrants, their families, as well as their communities. In this instance, mass awareness-raising programs using multiple media, preemployment orientation (PEO) and digital information, and in particular PDO are important information-delivery tools. PDO can help migrants with decision-making related to migration and ensuring family welfare, as well as provide information on existing available services, health, remittance management, realities of living and working in destination countries, and equipping migrants with the life skills necessary to deal with their day-to-day life while abroad.

This report provides short-term recommendations for deported migrants and migrants in the reentry ban list of the Russian Federation in terms of immediate assistance. For all categories of returning migrants deported or voluntary, the report recommends medium- and long-term recommendations. Some of these recommendations include developing a return policy, early-warning mechanisms for Tajik migrant workers with reentry bans, legal aid services, and other concerns.

Further recommendations focus on the need to develop skills training based on international standards, provide language training, and recognize already-acquired skills. Closely linked to these factors are the need to explore new labor markets and create overseas employment opportunities for destination countries other than CIS. With Tajikistan's mountainous terrain and a majority of its migrants coming from rural areas, providing information digitally will be cost-effective for migrants. Digitization of migration services and expansion of the dissemination of information through digital means are recommended to not only increase coverage but also widen its span. Some services, for example, registration, can also be provided digitally. This report also stresses short-, medium-, and long-term recommendations to deal with the COVID-19 pandemic.

The report takes a deep dive into the challenges of migration, but its advantages should not be minimized—migration is an important livelihood option for Tajik citizens. Addressing the challenges will bring even further positive outcomes for the migrants, their families, the community, and ultimately the country.

Introduction and Methodology

Background and Rationale: Over the past decade, Tajikistan has steadily reduced poverty and expanded its economy. Between 2000 and 2017, the poverty rate declined from 83% to 30% of the population, while the economy grew at an average rate of 7% per year.[1] After the civil war (1992–1997), newly established political stability and foreign aid have allowed the country's economy to expand with its GDP growth rate among the highest in neighboring countries (MOU, MOLME-ADB 2019). A major driving force of this economic growth is international labor migration. Once a part of the former Soviet Union, labor migration is no new phenomenon in Tajikistan. However, since independence, the Tajik economy has increased its reliance on migration and remittance. From the Soviet era to date, the Russian Federation remains the major destination for Tajik migrants. Remittances from labor migrants are equivalent to about a third of the country's GDP.

In the last decade, remittances from labor migration to Tajikistan have fluctuated, from 27% to 44% in the equivalent of the country's GDP. Between 2011 and 2013, remittances as measured compared to GDP were above 40%, with 2013 reaching the highest value (43.8%).[2] However, because of the Russian Federation's economic slowdown, new migration regulations, and the devaluation of its national currency, many Tajik migrants did not find it economically advantageous to continue to work in the Russian Federation (JICA 2019). Between 2014 and 2019, remittances as a percentage of GDP were from 27% to 37% (approximate value) (footnote 1).

International migration is an important livelihood option for many households in developing countries, including Tajikistan. The total value of remittances far exceeds that of official development assistance for many developing countries and even exceeds the value of foreign direct investment (FDI) for some. Remittance significantly supplements foreign currency reserves in many countries as well. In 2017, remittance in Tajikistan was almost equivalent to 30% (ADB 2019a) of the GDP, foreign direct investment net inflows were reported at 2.6% of GDP,[3] and official development assistance was 3.7% of gross national income.[4]

International migration provides employment, income, and foreign currency reserves for economies; however, it affects social dynamics. With a large number of citizens of working-age population, particularly men, absent from home for a few months to a year, women take on more responsibilities in managing the household and become decision-makers. In 2019, nearly 21.5% of the labor force left officially for work abroad,[5] whereas the percentage of remittance compared to national GDP was 33.4% (ADB 2020). Tajik migration brings both new opportunities and challenges for the government and policy-makers within agencies supporting the government efforts. A major concern for the government is managing the outflow of migrant workers while ensuring their safety, rights, and welfare.

---

[1]   World Bank. *Tajikistan* (accessed on 19 February 2020).
[2]   World Bank. *Personal Remittances, received (% of GDP) — Tajikistan* (accessed on 19 February 2020).
[3]   The Global Economy. *Tajikistan: Foreign Direct Investment, percent of GDP* (accessed on 24 January 2020).
[4]   World Bank; *Net ODA Received (% of GNI)* (accessed on 24 January 2020).
[5]   2019 data: Total labor force was 2,464,952 (Source: ILOSTAT database, retrieved on 1 March 2020. Cited in World Bank. *Labor force, total—Tajikistan.* https://data.worldbank.org/indicator/SL.TLF.TOTL.IN?locations=TJ [accessed 20 April 2020]) and total migration was 530,883 (Source: Annual Press Conference with mass media on 6 February 2020, at 2 pm. Data cited by the Honorable Minister, MOLME Gulru Jabborzoda).

The economic crisis brought on by the coronavirus disease (COVID-19) pandemic and the ensuing shutdown worldwide have changed international migration flows; global remittances are projected to decline by 7.0% in 2020.[6] However, in Europe and Central Asia, remittances are estimated to fall by as much as 28% due to the combined effect of the global COVID-19 pandemic and lower oil prices (World Bank 2020).

Lockdowns, travel bans, and social distancing have halted global economic activities. Host countries face additional challenges in many sectors, such as health and agriculture, that depend on the availability of migrant workers.[7] Migrants, on the other hand, face the risk of contagion and may lose employment, health insurance coverage, and employment visas (KNOMAD 2020).

Before the pandemic, labor migrants faced challenges in moving to a new country where culture, traditions, and practices differ from those of their home countries. In focus group discussions (FGDs) with Tajik labor migrants for this study, the migrants cited language, laws, skills, and cultural adjustment as major problems they face in the destination countries. Migrants and stakeholders emphasized adjusting to work and living conditions as a major challenge. Migrants also identified that adjustment is more difficult for first-time migrants.

To assist labor migrants to adjust with relative ease in the destination countries, many countries provide predeparture orientation (PDO) programs that deliver vital information about the life, culture, language, and laws in the destination countries. It also informs migrants of their rights and responsibilities and services provided by governments (both origin and destination countries) and civil society organizations (CSOs). Some long-established good practices on PDOs are found in Bangladesh, Indonesia, Nepal, the Philippines, and Sri Lanka.

The PDO programs often include premigration decision-making programs, preemployment programs, and awareness-raising programs on safe migration in the form of community-based programs and/or nationwide campaigns. Predeparture programs may also include migration loan facilities, skills training, and language training.

Post-return services are equally important and can begin with providing airport service after return; legal, psychological, and economic support; and easily obtained, low-interest loans for investing in the home country.

In recent years, governments are taking advantage of advanced information and communication technology in training and information dissemination through mobile applications and websites. Digitization of information poses its difficulties and advantages. However, for labor-origin countries like Tajikistan, it can be a practical and inexpensive tool to reach labor migrants. During the ongoing COVID-19 pandemic, wherein social distancing is vital to control COVID-19 infections, digital tools can play a significant role in informing and educating migrant workers.

Understanding that reliance on migration will not reduce in the short term, the Government of Tajikistan has taken some steps in making migration beneficial for migrants and their families and ensuring their social protection.

Objective: To support the Government of Tajikistan in its effort to strengthen services to migrant workers, this report aims to achieve the following:

i)   review the state of international migration out of Tajikistan, including its history, estimated numbers of outgoing migrants, destinations, duration/frequencies, occupations, remittance and the economic impacts, problems associated with working abroad, problems facing returning migrant and their families, and existing migration management structure and services available in the country;

ii) review international good practices of predeparture services including PDO provided by government agencies for international migrants;

---

[6]   Ratha, Dilip et al. 2020. Phase II: COVID-19 Crisis through a Migration Lens. Migration and Development Brief 33. Washington, DC: KNOMAD-World Bank. https://www.knomad.org/sites/default/files/2020-11/Migration%20%26%20Development_Brief%2033.pdf.

[7]   KNOMAD. 2020. *COVID-19 Crisis: Through a Migration Lens.* Migration and Development Brief 32. Washington, DC.

iii) review good practices of post-return services;

iv) identify the impacts of the COVID-19 pandemic on Tajikistan international migration and remittance; and

v) propose appropriate predeparture programs and post-return services for Tajik migrants.

Methodology: The methodology of the assessment is based on the review of primary and secondary sources. Primary data and information were collected from interviews with key stakeholders and migrants from a field visit to Dushanbe over 3–7 February 2020. The migrants were interviewed at the Pre-Departure Center for Migrants in Dushanbe selected at random from the migrants who came for assistance due to being placed on the reentry ban list of the Russian Federation.[8] A list of persons interviewed is attached as Appendix 1 of the report. Secondary data include a review of existing literature on Tajik migration, other relevant issues, and existing predeparture training courses provided by the Government of Tajikistan. A glossary of terms is also provided.

Limitation of the Report: This study uses a qualitative strategy for primary data collection. The migrants interviewed for the study and the reports reviewed focus on Tajik migrants' experience in the Russian Federation. Little to no information was available on other destination countries (Germany, Italy, Kazakhstan, Republic of Korea, Romania, Turkey, United Arab Emirates, and other countries). Two FGDs were implemented with migrants who were in the reentry ban list to the Russian Federation. No women migrants were available during the field visit, so none could be interviewed. All data concerning women migrants and family members were gathered from stakeholder interviews and secondary data. The primary data recorded by the government provide the numbers of migrants by gender and destination country. However, data on the number of meetings held by different government agencies for the migrant workers could not be collected as they are not centralized and many crucial data remain at the *jamoat* and/or district level.[9]

---

[8] A list of migrants who have been issued reentry bans for breach of the Russian Federation's administrative regulations or violation of other laws.

[9] The *jamoats* of Tajikistan are the third-level administrative divisions, similar to communes or municipalities. There are 405 *jamoats* in the country. Each *jamoat* is further subdivided into villages. (https://en.wikipedia.org/wiki/Jamoats_of_Tajikistan).

Migration in Tajikistan: Overview, Management, and Services

General Information: Tajikistan

Tajikistan is the smallest country in Central Asia, with a total land area of 144,510 square kilometers according to the The World Factbook of the Central Intelligence Agency (CIA).[10] It borders the Kyrgyz Republic to the north, the People's Republic of China to the east, Afghanistan to the south, and Uzbekistan to the west and northwest. Tajikistan is administratively divided into four regions or oblasts:

- Dushanbe (capital) and Regional Republic Subordination, which consist of 13 autonomous districts, is located in the central part of the country;

- Sughd Oblast is situated in the north;

- Khatlon Oblast is in the southwest; and

- Gorno-Badakhshan ("Mountain Badakhshan") Autonomous Oblast (GBAO) is located in the eastern part of the country. The autonomous region's capital is Khorugh (Khorog).

Only about 6% of the land is available for agricultural production.[11] Khatlon is the main region for agricultural production, followed by Sugdh (ADB 2019a).

Tajikistan is ethnically diverse with an estimated population of 9.1 million, of which Tajik is 84.3% (includes Pamiri and Yagnobi), Uzbek 13.8%, and others 2% (includes Kyrgyz, Russian, Turkmen, Tatar, Arab)—estimated as of 2014; languages spoken in the country include Tajik (official) at 84.4%, Uzbek 11.9%, Kyrgyz 0.8%, Russian 0.5%, and others 2.4%—estimated as of 2010 (Central Asia: Tajikistan—The World Factbook).

Although the population density of Tajikistan is 56 persons per square kilometer,[12] the population is unevenly distributed across regions because of its mountainous landscape and population concentrated in the valleys. About one fourth of the population lives in urban areas (Central Asia: Tajikistan—The World Factbook). Tajikistan also has a comparatively large young population, and population projections indicate that the trend will continue in the next 2 decades (ADB 2019a).

Historical and Cultural Ties in Relation to International Migration

During the Soviet period, population flows went two ways. The proportion of Russians among Tajikistan's population grew from less than 1% in 1926 to 13% in 1959.[13] The Russian immigrants came, some by force and some by choice, to work in the cotton industry and to take positions in the government.[14] In addition to the changing ethnic composition in

---

[10] For more details on Tajikistan's country profile, please see ADB. 2019a. Skills and Employability Enhancement Project (SEEP), Republic of Tajikistan; TA Draft Final Report. pp. 3–11.

[11] TajStat, 2015: Tajikistan in Figures. Dushanbe. According to the ADB, a quarter of Tajikistan's total land area (14 million ha) is agricultural land; however, in 2010, less than one-fifth of agricultural land was classified as arable. Quoted in ADB. 2019a. p. 3.

[12] TajStat, 2015: Tajikistan in Figures. Dushanbe. Quoted in ADB. 2019a. p. 2.

[13] Tajikistan — Ethnic Groups Archived 7 December 2010 at the Wayback Machine, U.S. Library of Congress. Quoted in Wikipedia; Tajikistan. https://en.wikipedia.org/wiki/Tajikistan (accessed on 20 January 2020).

[14] MPI. 2006. Tajikistan: From Refugee Sender to Labor Exporter. Migration Information Source. 1 July. https://www.migrationpolicy.org/article/tajikistan-refugee-sender-labor-exporter.

Tajikistan, the Soviet authorities forced many ethnic Tajik communities to be relocated within Tajikistan to supply agricultural labor (MPI 2006). It also included the unorganized resettlement of factory workers and mill hands, the organized resettlement of deported nations, the evacuation of populations during World War II, and the mobilization of young people for construction projects.[15]

In addition, the local youth went to the Russian Federation and Ukraine for vocational training and higher education during the 1970s and 1980s. Many enlisted soldiers also settled in the Russian Federation after completing their military service there, particularly in the Khabarovsk region and the Russian Federation's far east. Another large-scale migration occurred during the organized recruitment for the oil and gas fields in eastern Siberia (IOM 2003).

After the fall of the Soviet Union in 1991, a civil war occurred between 1992 and 1997. The civil war led nearly all ethnic minorities to emigrate and created massive demographic upheaval (MPI 2006). During the civil war, Tajiks fell back on older forms of belonging, while Islam remained important to many Tajiks, the form of membership that dominated was the *avlod* or clan (IOM 2003). Clan allegiance determined where people fled, and many ethnic Tajiks returned to their mountainous, ancestral villages (IOM 2003).

The aftermath of the civil war saw refugee resettlement, but nearly all of the ethnic minorities that fled Tajikistan during the civil war did not return (MPI 2006). During the Tajik civil war, many refugees settled in CIS countries, particularly the Russian Federation. Over the years, they settled in their host countries and became involved in economic activities. They played a significant role in determining the migration flow (IOM 2003).

After the civil war, lack of economic opportunities at home and instability pushed many Tajiks to seek employment overseas. Many young people found themselves without job opportunities or any reasonable prospects for the future, and labor migration provided a safety valve to release the pressures of social discontent and possible unrest.[16] An overwhelming majority of the labor migrants sought employment in the Russian Federation, where economic growth, comparatively high wages, ease of migration, and labor shortages have pulled Tajiks after the decade following the Tajik civil war (IOM 2003).

Social and Economic Context of Migration

Tajikistan's economy is not creating enough jobs for its rapidly growing labor force (ADB 2019a).[17] Fifty-five percent of the working-age population is not economically active as they do not participate in the labor force.[18] In 2017, Tajikistan had a labor force of 2.5 million, with 1.5 million employed in the agricultural sector and a registered unemployed population of 53,000.[19] In 2013, the proportion of women in the workforce stood at only 27%, compared to 63% for men (ADB 2019a). In addition, more than half of the country's workforce is underemployed (ADB 2019c), and half of the workforce has informal jobs that could be defined as jobs for which employers do not pay social tax; consequently, the employees will not receive pension (JICA 2019).

According to the JICA Household Report (2019), 55% of migrants did not work until they left for migration, and 10% left after graduating from schools. The main reason quoted in the study to go abroad was job search (92%), family reasons (4%), and study (2%). Lack of job opportunities was quoted as a decisive reason for seeking employment opportunities abroad (JICA 2018). Low wages in the domestic market was

[15]   IOM. 2003. *Labour Migration from Tajikistan*. Dushanbe.
[16]   University of Sussex. 2007. *Migration and Poverty Reduction in Tajikistan*. Development Research Centre on Migration, Globalisation and Poverty. Working Paper C11. Brighton.
[17]   For more details on economy and labor force, please see ADB. 2019a. Skills and Employability Enhancement Project (SEEP), Republic of Tajikistan; TA Draft Final Report. pp. 18–33 and JICA. 2019. Migration, Living Conditions and Skills: Panel Study Tajikistan Survey. pp. 20–23.
[18]   JICA. 2019. *Forthcoming Report on Household Survey: Migration, Living Conditions and Skills: Panel Study—Tajikistan*, 2018. Tokyo.
[19]   ADB. 2019c. *Key Indicators for Asia and the Pacific 2019*; Tajikistan. https://data.adb.org/dataset/tajikistan-key-indicators (accessed on 20 January 2020).

also another major push factor for migration. Some young men also report leaving for the lure of big cities in preference to small communities in rural Tajikistan; others, according to stakeholders, leave for overseas employment to avoid being enlisted in military service.

Other than lack of employment opportunities at home, migration is planned as a solution to personal socioeconomic problems (accumulate funds for business, land, house, car, capital, wedding, and study; response to material/fund crisis; invest in children's future) and improving job opportunities.[20] The Russian Federation is the major destination country for Tajik migrants. Visa-free and/or on-arrival visa options in the region and easy communication also make it easier for migrants to seek overseas employment within the region.

Trends and Patterns

According to various research carried out over the years, Tajik migration is predominantly seasonal; migrants typically leave Tajikistan for construction, agricultural, or other types of work during the short summer period (March/April to October/November) and return home.[21] However, the statistics do not indicate whether a recorded migrant worker is crossing borders for seasonal, temporary, or permanent jobs.

Flow of Migration

In the past 5 years, about half a million Tajiks annually left the country for overseas employment (Table 1). The majority of labor migrants are men. Large male representation can be explained by the fact that the host countries (in particular the Russian Federation) have a strong demand for "male occupations" as well as the prevailing perception in Tajikistan that men should be the breadwinners.[22]

The number of Tajik migrants in the Russian Federation in irregular status remains unclear. In an International Organization for Migration (IOM) study, the number of citizens of Tajikistan who were placed on the migration register in the Russian Federation for the purpose of "work" between 2009 and 2019 was 936,800.[23] The Japan International Cooperation Agency (JICA) Survey (2018) estimates that 780,829 were international migrants working and living abroad, which would be about 14% of the labor force. The Migration Policy Institute (MPI) estimates that about 800,000 migrants work in the Russian Federation (MPI 2019).

Table 1:   Number of Migrant Workers by Gender (2015–2019)

Year	2015	2016	2017	2018	2019
Total number of migrants	551,728	517,308	487,757	484,176	530,883
Number of male migrants	487,137	435,457	419,721	419,664	453,870
Percentage of male migrants	88.3	84.2	86.1	86.7	85.5
Number of female migrants	64,591	81,851	68,036	64,512	77,013
Percentage of female migrants	11.7	15.8	13.9	13.3	14.5

Source: 2015–2018 data: TajStat Labor Market in the Republic of Tajikistan (up to 2018), Dushanbe. Quoted in *TA 9639-TAJ: Skills and Employability Enhancement Project, Republic of Tajikistan*.

2019 data: Annual Press Conference with mass media on 6 February 2020, at 2 pm. Data cited by the Honorable Minister, MOLME Gulru Jabborzoda.

---

[20] IOM. 2019c. *External Youth Migration in the Countries of Central Asia: Risk Analysis and Minimization of Negative Consequences.* Kazakhstan.

[21] For further details on trends and patterns of migration from Tajikistan, please see JICA. 2019. *Household Survey: Migration, Living Conditions and Skills: Panel Study—Tajikistan, 2018.* Pp. 16–19 and ADB. 2019a. *Skills and Employability Enhancement Project (SEEP), Republic of Tajikistan; TA Draft Final Report.*

[22] ETF Migration Survey. 2010. p. 23. Quoted in ADB. 2019a. *Skills and Employability Enhancement Project, Republic of Tajikistan.* p. 36.

[23] Statistical information on the migration situation. Website of the Ministry of Internal Affairs of the Russian Federation. Quoted in IOM. 2019c. *External Youth Migration in the Countries of Central Asia: Risk Analysis and Minimization of Negative Consequences.* Kazakhstan. https://publications.iom.int/system/files/pdf/external_youth_migration_en.pdf.

Countries of Employment

Tajik migrants' major destination country is the Russian Federation (97.6%).[24] Other destination countries include Germany, Kazakhstan, the Kyrgyz Republic, the Republic of Korea, Turkey, the United States, United Arab Emirates, and Uzbekistan (JICA 2019). Many factors play in the Russian Federation being the major destination. The Tajikistan–Russian Federation shared past governance, language commonalities, mutually recognized university degrees/diplomas, visa-free entry, significant wage differentials (for unskilled work, monthly wage compared to $78 in Tajikistan might be $281 in the Russian Federation),[25] and existing migrant network and experience, which are major reasons why Tajikistan's labor migrants choose the Russian Federation as their destination country (JICA 2018).

Before the economic slowdown in the Russian Federation, its growing economy attracted immigrant workers from other parts of the post-Soviet space, especially from less-developed central Asian countries.

In the 2000s, the Russian Federation's percentage of total immigrant flows rose from 24.4% (2000–2004) to 33.5% (2005–2009) and to 40.4% in 2010–2013.[26] Large macroeconomic turbulence in the Russian Federation in 2014, devaluation of the national currency, and the 2015 change in the Russian Federation's migration policy affected Tajik migration to the Russian Federation (JICA 2019). As a result, the number of migrants working in the Russian Federation started declining from 2014 and consequently the size of remittances decreased to 2.3 billion US dollars in 2017, which is equivalent to 32% of Tajikistan's GDP (JICA 2019). However, in 2019, 16% more migrants left for the Russian Federation to work compared to 2018.[27] On the other hand, overseas employment in Kazakhstan decreased by 24% (2019) compared to 2018.

Tajik migrant workers can be found in practically all Russian regions, with large concentrations in the megacities (Moscow, Moscow region, St. Petersburg), as well as in the regions bordering or close to Kazakhstan: Sverdlovsk, Novosibirsk, Tyumen, Samara, Chelyabinsk, and Kemerovo regions, Krasnoyarsk Territory (DRCM 2007).

Figure 1:   Occupation before Migration

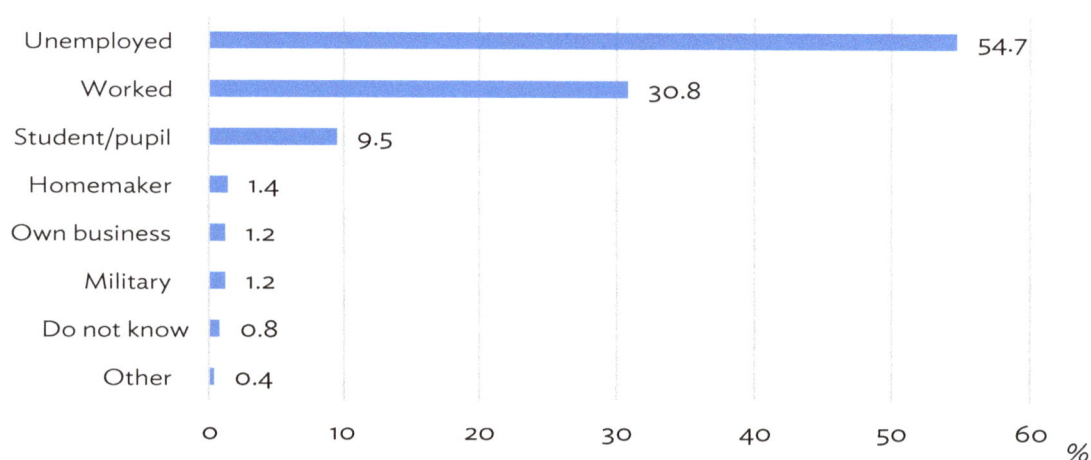

Source: Authors' calculations using JICA. 2018. *Migration, Living Conditions & Skills: Panel Study—Tajikistan Survey* quoted in JICA. 2019. *Household Survey: Migration, Living Conditions and Skills: Panel Study — Tajikistan.* p. 25.

---

24   Annual Press Conference with mass media, 6 February 2020, at 2 pm. Data cited by the Honorable Minister, MOLME Gulru Jabborzoda.
25   ADB. 2019a. p. 36.
26   European University Institute (EUI). 2014. *Regional Migration Report: Russia and Central Asia.* Migration Policy Centre (MPC). Fiesole.
27   Annual Press Conference with mass media, 6 February 2020, at 2 pm. Data cited by the Honorable Minister, MOLME Gulru Jabborzoda.

Individual Characteristics of Tajik Migrants

Migration from Tajikistan is male dominated. The largest group of migrants is 15–29 years old (45.4%) followed by the group aged 30–44 (39.5%) (JICA 2019). Although in 2019 female migration increased by double the increase in male migration (24% increase, compared to 12% increase in male labor migrants), women's participation in labor migration has remained between 12% and 16% in the last 5 years (footnote 26). In addition, for both genders, the majority were unemployed before migrating, as shown in Figure 1 (JICA 2019).

IOM (2003) identified that 75% of Tajik migrants spoke Russian in addition to their native language; however, knowledge of a second or third language is more common among older people than the younger generation. The younger the migrant worker, the lower the level of their language skills.

More than 85% of the labor migrants were from rural areas (JICA 2018). Roughly 75% of the migration is seasonal, meaning that the migrants return to Tajikistan at least once a year (JICA 2018). Tajik migration of seasonal workers often occurs in groups. It is standard practice for construction brigades and artels (associations) of agricultural workers to live under the laws of the clan or *avlod*.[28] According to an IOM study (IOM 2003), the foreman plays the role of the head of the *avlod*. He exercises undisputed authority over the brigade. The brigade is often formed based on family and regional ties.

Role of Migrant Networks

Migrant networks are webs of social ties that connect individuals from a sending region to others in a receiving context. Research shows that these networks influence the magnitude and direction of migration flows from the sending region as well as migrants' adaptation outcomes in the destination.[29] Migrant networks increase the social capital of migrants.

Migration networks are an important factor in labor migration in Tajikistan; they impact migration magnitude, job search, adaptation, and sending remittances (JICA 2019). Existence of migrant networks and previous migration experience plays a major role in selecting destination countries. The presence of relatives and friends in the country of destination is one of the pull factors that facilitate travel abroad for employment (JICA 2019). According to the results of a JICA study (2019), 38% of respondents cited the existence of relatives and 18% cited friends for selecting the destination country while 17% cited their previous migration experience. These experienced migrants also become a source of information for the new generation of migrants (JICA 2019).

Acquiring Skills before Departure

According to the JICA survey report (2019), for 58% of the surveyed returned migrants, the skills (work experience and training) acquired in their own country were useful in finding employment. At the same time, 85% of those who intend to migrate noted that the formal education they received will help them find jobs abroad. However, 50.4% of returned migrants believe that there is no need for professional education in

---

[28] *Avlod* can be loosely translated as clan. According to an IOM study (2003), "the influence of the *avlod* on Tajik labor migration is difficult to overestimate. In Tajik society, an *avlod* (also known as *qaymi* or *toyfa*) is a patriar-chal community of blood relatives who have a common ancestor and common interests, and, in many cases, shared property and means of production, and consolidated or coordinated household budgets. The institution is still widespread in rural areas. Vestiges are also present in the cities." *Avlod* wields enormous authority over the behavior of its individual members, and this institution determines the internal structure of labor migration. The initial decision-making process begins with family. Once a decision has been reached, it is discussed and confirmed by the *avlod* elders.

This traditional Tajik phenomenon was further strengthened by the aftermath of the civil war, when ethnore-gional groups were consolidated. In the postwar environment of weak government control, political instability, and lawlessness, people sought refuge and protection in their own ethnoregional group. To a certain extent, ethnoregional solidarity makes up the gap in social services in Tajikistan since the collapse of the education, public health, and social welfare systems (IOM 2003).

[29] Garip and Asad. 2015. *Migrant Networks*. Emerging Trends in the Social and Behavioral Sciences: An Interdisciplinary, Searchable, and Linkable Resource: 1–13. doi: 10.1002/9781118900772.etrds0220.

finding jobs abroad. The migrants interviewed in FGDs did not think it is necessary to develop skills in Tajikistan and hoped to develop skills in the Russian Federation.

However, migration experts in Tajikistan believe that improved job and language skills will increase the prospects of Tajik migrant workers in the destination countries. One of the reasons cited by the experts is the lack of knowledge among potential migrants on opportunities and advantages of skill-based migration. In addition, multiple stakeholders have stressed the importance of and need for modernizing existing skills training as well as improving training to the level of international standards.

Employment Sectors

A majority of the migrant men find work in the construction sector primarily as unskilled laborers. The majority of women who migrate find work in the service sector.

Analyzing Table 2, the migrant workers chose to work mainly in construction (59%), followed by trade and services (17%), manufacturing (5%), transport and communication (5%), and other (14%) sectors. These tend to be lower-paying positions. The types of job migrants engage in depend largely on the migrants' social capital (JICA 2019).

The type of work in migration does not necessarily depend on the qualifications and skills of migrant workers. Migrant respondents in the research mentioned that they worked in whichever job was available—construction, taxi driver, agriculture; their occupation often did not match their skill sets. About 28.3% of the recorded migrant workers were abroad for up to 6 months, 27.1% up to 1 year, and 44.6% for more than 1 year (ADB 2019a). The agricultural and construction season in the Russian Federation runs from April to October, accounting a higher flow of out-migration in March and April.

Table 2:   Distribution of Tajik Migrants Working in the Russian Federation, by Industry

Industry Sector	Men (%)	Women (%)	Total (%)
Construction	65	11	59
Wholesale, retail trade, hotels, restaurants	13	54	17
Manufacturing	5	4	5
Transport, storage, communication	6	2	5
Other communal and personal services	4	14	5
Agriculture, hunting, fishing, forestry	4	3	4
Education	0.5	4	1
Health and social services	0.5	3	1
Public administration and defense	1	3	1
Others	2	2	2

Source: TajStat Migration Survey. 2010; quoted in ADB; *TA 9639-TAJ: Skills and Employability Enhancement Project,* Republic of Tajikistan, p. 36.

Legal Status in Destination Countries

According to the *IOM World Migration Report 2020,* irregular migration is a feature in Central Asia, although exact numbers are difficult to ascertain. Weak border management and the remoteness of border areas have sustained the irregular forms of migration across the subregion. Visa-free regimes and on-arrival visa options for many CIS countries make it difficult to calculate exact numbers of migrants with irregular status. A migrant may enter the country legally and obtain permission to work; however, he or she may not renew this permission, which renders the migrant irregular. Since no work patent or permit or other documents are required for Tajik migrants to stay in the Russian Federation for 90 days, some seasonal migrants work for 3 months and then come back home and return for another 3 months during the summer period to avoid incurring irregular status.

Migrants become irregular and are added to the reentry ban list of the Russian Federation for many reasons, ranging from minor administrative to serious offenses. Tajik citizens can enter the Russian Federation legally under a visa-free regime requiring only a valid passport. However, if the stay in the Federation exceeds 90 days and if work is intended, further steps need to be taken to not slip into irregularity.[30] Irregularity may occur for a range of reasons, and many migrant workers do not take the necessary steps required to obtain a legal work patent (footnote 31).

A migrant worker may become irregular for
(i) employment without recruitment permit;
(ii) working with expired or fraudulent documents;
(iii) different work than stated in the permit or patent;
(iv) entrepreneurial or independent labor activity without corresponding permits, licenses, and appropriate registration in the state bodies and also under false or expired documents; and
(v) involvement in illegal activities (IOM 2003).

Remittance

Tajikistan is one of the world's top five remittance-recipient countries measured by its relative size to GDP (IOM 2019b). In 2019, remittance amounted to $2.7 billion, which is equivalent to 33.4% of GDP.[31] Remittances from the Russian Federation have been substantial over time, aided by the relatively low transfer costs from the Russian Federation to the Central Asia countries (IOM 2019b). Among the factors behind this growth was the continued recovery of economic activity in the Russian Federation.

The remittances to Tajikistan help the migrants' families pay for their daily expenses and immediate needs.[32] Migrant families use an overwhelming portion of remittances (94%) for private consumption, which is the most important component of GDP.[33] However, remittances are rarely used for investments or to save for future contingencies.[34] In the 2010 International Labour Organization (ILO) household survey of 1,267 households, on saving remittance, 37% responded that they save no proportion of their income, while about 51% of the households manage to save up to 20%. About 9% report saving between 21 and 40%,

and about 3% report saving between 41% and 60% of their income. Interestingly, the survey reported that these savings are almost never kept in banks (98% of households having savings keep no portion of them in the banking sector). Of the households interviewed, 95% were aware of neither the saving products available nor their terms and conditions. Moreover, most of those who are aware of existing financial schemes do not keep their savings in banks because the amount is too small. The responses also indicated that this is compounded by a tradition of keeping savings at home and mistrust of banks (ILO 2010a).

The ILO survey also found that emigrants to Kazakhstan and the Russian Federation are more inclined to send remittances than those in other countries, regardless of the status of migration. On a positive note, 87% of migrants send remittances through official channels, that is, banks and money transfer organizations, and only 12% send money through other people (ILO 2010a). However, migrants still find the process of sending remittance difficult and the cost of transfer high. The average cost of sending $200 to Europe; the Central Asia region was 6.5% in 2019; the global cost of sending the same amount is 6.8% (World Bank 2020).

An IOM study (2019c) recorded the growth of dependent psychology as well, where the relatives and friends of migrant workers turn into consumers and do not seek to use the financial resources received for investment in the real sector of the economy. Lack of awareness of financial products and low trust in the banking sector is another reason for low investments. Trust in the banking system is generally low and the recent bankruptcy of two banks, Agroinvestbank and Tojiksodirotbank, will lead that trust to decrease even further.

---

30   IOM. 2014a. *Tajik Migrants with Re-entry Bans to the Russian Federation.* Dushanbe.
31   ADB. 2020a. *Asian Development Outlook 2020: What Drives Innovation in Asia?* Manila.
32   ILO. 2010a. *Migrant Remittances to Tajikistan: The Potential for Savings, Economic Investment and Existing Financial Products to Attract Remittances.* Moscow.
33   TajStat Migration Survey 2010; ETF Migration Survey 2010: 68.1% for household living expenses, 19.9% for renting the residence for the household, 17.8% for education, and only 5% for investment in businesses. Quoted in ADB. 2019a. p. 40.
34   Country Partnership Strategy quoting an ADB. Analysis of 2011; ILO Migrant Remittances to Tajikistan. According to TajStat Migration Survey 2010, only 11% are used for investment in durable goods, in real estate or in agriculture. Quoted in ADB. 2019a. p. 41.

In an FGD study, respondents cited too little money as a reason for not opening bank accounts. Most migrant workers in the FGD did not have a bank account.[35] Migrants also cited low salary as the main reason for lack of savings. The majority (80%–90%) of them mentioned that they invest in constructing houses or investing in a small flat.

Female Migration

In the last 5 years, women constituted approximately 12%–16% of international migration (TajStat). In 2019, women's participation rate in the labor force was 33%.[36] In the JICA Household Survey (2018), high unemployment among women was stressed by both male and female respondents. This was also related to the lack of childcare in rural areas, expensive fees for kindergartens, and the lack of employment opportunities for women (ADB 2019a).

However, female migration is gradually on the rise; in 2019, 77,013 women left for overseas employment, 24% more than in 2018.[37] Most women work in the service sector (cleaning, waitressing, elderly care, nanny, sellers, baking, and cooking) (JICA 2019). Migrant women work in better conditions than men because their service and trade-sector work is of a different nature (JICA 2019). Nonetheless, migrant women with professional education often work abroad according to their experience and education, but in low-paid and low-skilled jobs.

Some female migrants are in destination countries as dependents and therefore may not be employed (JICA 2019). A 2010 survey by the European Training Foundation found that 12.9% of labor migrants took their wives with them, for several reasons including needing help abroad, desire for children and family to be together, more advantageous financially, that is, in the event that migrants' wives were able to find jobs. However, it can be financially challenging for seasonal migrants to bring their family members with them (ETF 2010).

Issues of Concern in Labor Migration from Tajikistan

Challenges Faced by Migrants

A. Premigration preparation: Migrants identified lack of access to information and skills-training opportunities and high cost of migration (highest passport cost among CIS countries[38] and loans to pay for migration cost and maintaining family) as some of the problems in the premigration stage. Up to 85% of first-time migrants did not participate in training to obtain the skills necessary for jobs abroad.

The JICA study (2019) identified (interview of returned migrants) the following major steps undertaken by migrants during predeparture preparation (Figure 2): job search abroad (67%), information about the conditions of stay and residence in the country of destination (52%), and initial preparation of necessary documents for traveling abroad (49%). At the same time, 42% plan to improve their skills before departure.

Of first-time migrants, 85.5% report they never attended skills training, 54.0% did not acquire general information about migration, and 74.4% did not acquire specific contacts of their employers abroad (JICA 2019).

For predeparture preparation, migrants' (interview of 189 return migrants) sources of information were friends (40.2%), relatives (30.7%), family members (16.4%), other (4.8%), nongovernmental organizations (NGOs) (0.5%), individual brokers (0.5%), and newspaper advertisements (0.5%) (JICA 2019). The same study identified their village or *jamoat* as the main (66%) place of information gathering for

[35]   Interview with migrants (in the reentry ban list to the Russian Federation) 7 February 2020. .

[36]   ILOSTAT database. Data retrieved 1 March, 2020. Quoted in World Bank. *Labor Force Participation Rate, Female (% of female population ages 15-64) (modeled ILO estimate)—Tajikistan*. https://data.worldbank.org/indicator/SL.TLF.ACTI.FE.ZS?locations=TJ&name_desc=true (accessed on 20 February 2020).

[37]   Annual Press Conference with mass media on 6 February 2020, at 2 pm. Data cited by the Honorable Minister, MOLME Gulru Jabborzoda.

[38]   IOM. 2018b. *Return and Reintegration: Key Highlights*. Geneva.

Figure 2: Main Steps to Prepare for Migration, Returned Migrants

Step	%
Try to find a job abroad	67.0
Study the information on life conditions in your future	51.5
Legalize papers on a permanent residence abroad	48.5
Improve your qualifications	41.2
Register with the agency providing jobs abroad	29.9
Apply for a residence permit, a job, a student program	27.8
Learn a foreign language	23.7
Apply for a biometric passport	21.6
Apply for a visa	16.5
Address the experts holding emigration consultations	15.5
Try to sell (have sold) your property	10.3
Try to find a place to study abroad	9.3

Source: Authors' calculations based on JICA. 2018. *Migration, Living Conditions & Skills: Panel Study—Tajikistan Survey; and* JICA. 2019. *Report on Household Survey: Migration, Living Conditions and Skills: Panel Study—Tajikistan, 2018.* p. 30.

migrants. Neighboring villages (17.5%) was the second most frequent source of information followed by destination countries (16.5%).

B. Challenges at the destination country: The following are major challenges encountered at destination countries.

i) *Unemployment in migration:* Unemployment in migration has several features and legal consequences. Although many migrants secure a job in the destination country through friends and relatives, some migrants have no access to such networks. Unemployment for a period of 1–2 months significantly reduces the amount of earnings by migrants (JICA 2019). In the case of deportation, as the cost is also paid by the migrant workers themselves, the financial burden for an unsuccessful experience in migration falls on the shoulders of the migrant family (JICA 2019). Migrant workers often need to take a loan from relatives or friends to return to Tajikistan.

ii) *Difficulties in obtaining work patent and work permit in the Russian Federation:* In the Russian Federation, a work patent[39] allows a migrant worker to work for private individuals. To work in organizations and institutions, the migrant worker must obtain a work permit.[40] A quota system in the Russian Federation means that a significant number of migrant workers cannot obtain a work permit; therefore, they work for private companies on the basis of a patent. However, this practice is illegal and migrant workers can be administratively charged and fined from 2,000 to 5,000 rubles (approximately $27–66) in addition to administrative deportation from the Russian Federation.[41]

Also notable, for official employment, the recruiting organization must have a quota for foreign labor.[42] When the Russian Federation introduced the obligatory requirement for procurement of work permits that transferred the responsibility for legal employment to migrant workers, they turned into private entrepreneurs (JICA 2019). In addition, obtaining both a work permit and a work patent

---

[39]   A work patent is a document confirming the right of foreign citizens arriving in the Russian Federation on a visa-free basis (from Abkhazia, Azerbaijan, Moldova, Tajikistan, Ukraine, and Uzbekistan) to work in its territory (JICA 2019).

[40]   Art. 13.1 and 13.3 of the Federal Law of the Russian Federation No 114-FZ as of 25 July 2002 "On Legal Status of Foreign Citizens in the Russian Federation", quoted in Human Rights Center (HRC) 2014. *Legal Protection of Migrant Workers from Tajikistan in the Russian Federation.* Dushanbe.

[41]   Article 18.10 of the RF Code of Administrative Offences. Quoted in HRC. 2014.

[42]   HRC. 2014. *Legal Protection of Migrant Workers from Tajikistan in the Russian Federation.* Dushanbe.

requires a range of documents and visits to several government offices in the Russian Federation (JICA 2019).

iii) Work and living situation in destination countries: Newly arrived migrants in the Russian Federation receive support mainly from their relatives and friends in applying for employment, with 86% of respondents (international migrants) reporting that they relied on friends and relatives when applying for employment in the destination country (JICA 2019). Such social capital in the destination country becomes a source for finding a place of residence, preparing paperwork, sending remittances, and building connections (JICA 2019).

However, with or without the support of migrant networks—the majority of the migrants are low skilled, economically desperate, willing to accept any working conditions, nearly illiterate in terms of legal fluency, and limited in their language skills (HRC 2014). These conditions result in migrants becoming victims of labor exploitation by employers and police abuse and extortion by criminal gangs.[43] Xenophobic attitudes in the Russian Federation have been cited in the interviews of the returned migrants as one of the major difficulties of working there.

Police abuse of authority has been identified in a number of studies including extorting money (destroying documents and taking away passports, if unable to pay), verbal and physical abuse during documentation check, and detention if not in possession of passport and other documentation.[44] Notably, according to the FGD participants, those migrant workers who do not speak Russian are exposed to the biggest risk when facing police abuse.

"I will have to pay the police regardless of whether I have documentation or not, so why

bother."—Interview with a migrant worker on 4 February 2020.

Heavy, dangerous work and poor living conditions can lead to disease, injury, and even death. A majority of the migrant workers live and work in very bad and harsh conditions, which negatively affect their health (IOM 2003). Migrants tend to live together in overcrowded apartments. The major reason for this is the financial inability to afford proper housing and cost-minimization strategy. Other reasons for this practice include safety in numbers, fear of police raids, and security concerns of the neighborhood. Overcrowding results in health concerns, in particular, for infectious and communicable diseases. The current COVID-19 pandemic has made the situation more difficult for migrants.

A migrant needs health insurance to visit a physician; since many lack insurance, they try to self-care instead of going to the doctor. In serious cases, they will go to clinics that they cannot afford, resulting in debt.

Sexually responsible behavior is little understood among Tajik migrants, as sex outside marriage is considered a taboo. When people engage in nonmarital sexual relations, they fail to use methods of contraception and practice safe sex, thereby increasing the risk of unwanted pregnancy, infections, sexually transmitted diseases, and HIV/AIDS (IOM 2003). However, in recent times, information, education, and communication materials have been developed by different stakeholders to raise awareness about the risks of communicable diseases including HIV/AIDS and its different modes of transmission in government-run PDO programs. Nevertheless, more information sharing on communicable diseases is needed.

Social and psychological adaptation to the receiving countries is very difficult for many Tajik migrants (IOM

---

[43]   HRC. 2014. *Legal Protection of Migrant Workers from Tajikistan in the Russian Federation.* Dushanbe and MOU between MOLME and ADB for TA 9639-TAJ: The Skills and Employability Enhancement Project (SEEP). TRTA Final Review/Grant Fact Finding Mission. 4–19 November 2019.

[44]   IOM. 2003. *Labor Migration from Tajikistan.* Dushanbe; University of Sussex. 2007. Development Research Centre on Migration, Globalisation and Poverty. Working Paper C11. *Migration and Poverty Reduction in Tajikistan.* Brighton, and HRC. 2014. *Legal Protection of Migrant Workers from Tajikistan in the Russian Federation.* Dushanbe.

2003). "Majority of the migrants originate from rural areas, who may have never even visited Dushanbe. Migration to the Russian Federation is a big jump for them, they need to acclimatize themselves to urban centers first."[45] They need to adapt to two distinct types of situations: (i) the socialization of adult rural migrants to an urban environment and (ii) adaptation to a society from which the migrants are separated by a considerable cultural gap, language, and religion (IOM 2003).

Construction brigades have less contact with the receiving society; they create a semi-isolated micro-society that largely mitigates the need for adaptation in the destination countries (IOM 2003). In addition, police harassment also discourages migrants from traveling to city centers; therefore, Tajik migrants mostly live by themselves and do not integrate with the local population of the destination countries.

iv) Shortage of MOLME representatives at the destination countries: The Ministry of Labor, Migration and Employment (MOLME) or the Migration Service representatives are responsible for the issues that are outside the scope of competence of consular service, that is, facilitation in receiving salaries, assistance at detention or deportation of migrants, job counseling, and legalization of labor activity in the Russian Federation (HRC 2014). The positions were created in 2001 in response to abuses and difficulties faced by migrant workers in the Russian Federation (DRCM 2007). Representatives in St. Petersburg organized effective monitoring of the problems faced by migrant workers (HRC 2014). However, migrants are not always aware of the activities of these services in destination countries.

Stakeholders (including migrants) identified a lack of an adequate number of representatives in the destination countries as an obstacle in providing support to the migrant workers. For example, in the Russian Federation, the number of representatives is 16 to 18, with a migrant population of about 800,000 (estimated); therfore, it is impossible to provide support adequately. In addition, representatives do not

have diplomatic status, which is a barrier in carrying out their functions.

v) Access to legal aid: "Migrant workers from Tajikistan, whose rights are violated in the territory of the Russian Federation, are in a difficult situation due to the limited access to legal remedies in the Russian Federation. They practically do not seek help from the state bodies of the Russian Federation due to the lack of documented status of their stay or because of mistrust. Their access to consular protection provided by the Republic of Tajikistan in the Russian Federation is limited, as a rule, because of the difficulties associated with physical access to them" (HRC 2014).

In case of grievances, with or without legal documentation, migrants first contact intermediaries or the diaspora (who in turn forward it to the intermediaries). They will contact NGOs, the Migration Service of Tajikistan, Consulate, and Embassy only if negotiations fail (HRC 2014).

In the 2014 Human Rights Center (HRC) study, migrants identified the following reasons for not seeking official government support: low awareness of the official institutions, lack of trust and expectations for the assistance and information support they can get in these institutions, and negative experiences with the official institutions of the Republic of Tajikistan in the Russian Federation. Migrants seek assistance from the NGOs at a low rate as well. The same study also revealed that the younger generation's other sources of information on legal issues included the internet. Older migrants reported that they receive information on TV, meeting with relatives and friends at weddings and other events, in the mosques, as well as communication with intermediaries.

C. Challenges of returning migrants and their families: Migrants can return for a number of reasons including mismatch of migrants' skills and employers' demand for skills, inability to find jobs, low wages, seasonality of work, family issues, and illness. For Tajik migrants, reasons also include policy changes in the Russian Federation and economic growth slowdown. The major challenge of return is related to economic,

---

[45]   Interview with Amirbekzooda Mehrobsho, deputy director, Agency of Labor and Employment.

social, and psychosocial reintegration needed to maintain life, livelihood and dignity, and inclusion in civic life.

i) Economic reintegration: Many returning migrants experience difficulty in finding a suitable job due to the poor employment opportunities in their home country and because the skills acquired abroad are either not relevant to the Tajik labor market or not acknowledged. An IOM study on the situation of migrants banned from returning to the Russian Federation found that some 24% of the migrants stated that their families now have difficulties affording enough food, and 33% report that although their income is sufficient for food, it hardly allows them to buy new clothes and other daily necessities (JICA 2019).

Unemployment, in addition, largely depends on the origin of the migrant workers. A study[46] conducted in the GBAO region examined the potential of the returning migrants to be employed in the domestic market, revealing that only about one third of the existing returnees would be able to find employment in the region given the scarcity of job opportunities.

The research also shows that jobs advertised through the state employment agency do not fully reflect the local labor market because not all employers send information about vacancies to the Labor and Employment Agency, and the advertised vacancies are usually for poorly paid work (CSCG 2016).

Many migrants return home with skills acquired abroad; however, either there is no need for that specific skill set in Tajikistan or there is very little option for skill recognition. In some cases, migrants are not aware of skill recognition procedures/options.

"I have skills, I just need someone to give me a certificate that will be recognized."— Interview with a migrant worker on 7 February 2020.

ii) Social reintegration is the access by a returning migrant to public services and infrastructures in his or her country of origin, including access to health, education, housing, justice, and social protection schemes (IOM 2019a). In the study, lack of social protection after return has been identified as an issue by migrants and migration experts.

The Tajik pension legislation affects longstanding labor migrants and what personal strategies would ensure a dignified retirement for the migrants. There is also debate about what policy reforms should be adopted. Currently, pension is formulated on the basis of a citizen's last 15 years of official employment and rates of his or her salary confirmed by employers. It confirms that a citizen has paid into the pension fund. If there is no such documentation, a citizen will automatically be given a minimal rate of pension after retirement. The study revealed that, given the seasonal nature of migrant workers' stay in Tajikistan and the often-unregistered labor arrangements, it is not feasible for most migrant workers to accumulate the legally required length of pensionable service. In general, Tajik migrant workers are almost universally unaware of the pension reform, and many of them expect to receive a much larger pension than the basic state social pension. This means that the majority of Tajik migrant workers constitute an at-risk group of people, whose expectations do not match reality. Most migrants see a way out of this problematic situation in the signing of an intergovernmental agreement between Tajikistan and the Russian Federation on social security for Tajik migrant workers, so they can accumulate national insurance contributions in the Russian Federation that can count toward their pension when they retire in Tajikistan. Although the Tajikistan government is taking steps to negotiate the signing of such an agreement, in the meantime, it has not taken any alternative decisive actions (CSCG 2016).

Stakeholders and migrant groups both stressed the importance of developing a process for accommodating migrant social tax in the state pension system. A number of migrants shared their frustration in the FGD saying "just fix the pension."

---

[46] Civil Society Contact Group (CSCG) Tajikistan. 2016. *Changing Patterns of Labor Migration in Tajikistan.* International Alert. March. https://www.international-alert.org/sites/default/files/Tajikistan_LaborMigrationPatterns_EN_2016.pdf.

iii) Psychosocial reintegration is defined as the reinsertion of a returning migrant into personal support networks (friends, relatives, and neighbors) and civil society structures (associations, self-help groups, and other organizations). This also includes the re-engagement with the values, way of living, language, moral principles, ideology, and traditions of the country of origin (IOM 2019a).

Economic and social reintegration problems are easily observed; challenges of psychosocial reintegration are less visible. The nature of work and living conditions of Tajik migrants (discussed in Challenges at the Destination Country) make for psychosocial reintegration with very few difficulties.

The main reason for this ease of reintegration is that the migration is seasonal, where migrants work only for 6 months of the year. In addition, living and working in groups, lack of adjustment to the host society owing to xenophobia, irregular status, and harassment by the police mean that most Tajik migrants never integrate into the host society. In addition, in this age of easy communication with family, via social media and communication tools, a migrant is never very far away from family or news of the home country.

Tajik culture and society remain an integral part of migrants' identity despite staying in the Russian Federation. In fact, because of the widespread xenophobic attitudes and prejudices against Central Asian migrant workers in the Federation, their home society often becomes an even stronger point of reference and part and parcel of their identity (IOM 2014a).

Psychosocial reintegration was perceived as problematic only in a minority of cases. In the IOM study carried out in 2014, 75% of the respondents said they were happy to be back in Tajikistan despite all the problems since it is, after all, their home and they could be close to their friends and family again.

When migrants have a family in the Russian Federation with a long separation, the reentry ban causes a psychosocial burden that leads to reintegration problems. Interviews with migrants in an FGD held on 4 February 2020 revealed that one migrant had a Russian wife, one had Russian citizenship and family and children, and one had parents in the Russian Federation. Psychosocial integration should be part of any orientation program with migrants, in particular, for deported migrants, migrants who have been in detention centers or prisons and migrants in the reentry ban list of the Russian Federation.

Overall, a study by Anvar Babaev confirms that the long-term absence of returning migrants significantly affects their social environment.[47] They lose contact with some relatives, friends, former colleagues, and acquaintances with whom they once had shared interests and contacts. Labor migrants are therefore usually unable to find employment by reaching out to friends and relatives as well as former employers, which is the typical way to get a job in Tajikistan.

Migrants in the Reentry Ban List of the Russian Federation

According to MOLME, as of December 2019, 267,324[48] Tajik migrants were banned from working in the Russian Federation. The list of banned migrant workers grows by approximately 20,000 every 3 months (ADB 2019a).

Research has shown that as many as 80% of the migrants banned from reentry to the Russian Federation did not know about their bans when they last left the country. Many of them found out about their ban only when they were turned down by Russian border guards upon their attempt to return to the Russian Federation as there is no regular mechanism to inform "offenders" about their status. In most cases, violation of the Russian Federation's migration procedures due to insufficient understanding of these caused the reentry ban, but there are also reports about working migrants who deliberately tried to stay under the authorities' radar by pretending to be tourists. At times, simple wrongdoings in the traffic and basic breaches of the law have been the cause of the reentry ban (ADB 2019a).

47   Babaev. 2016. *The Migration Situation in Tajikistan: Problems and Solutions.* Central Asian Bureau for Analytical Reporting. Quoted in ADB. 2019a.
48   Annual Press Conference with mass media on 6 February 2020, at 2 pm. Data cited by the Honorable Minister, MOLME Gulru Jabborzoda.

The ban on returning to the Russian Federation worsens the migrants' situation because many of their families rely entirely on the income earned abroad and most of the remittances are spent on household consumption. Also, since remittances are seldom saved or used for investing, returning migrants often experience serious problems starting their own business. Furthermore, the lack of sufficient startup capital makes it difficult to get access to preferential loans.

One solution to the plight of migrants on the reentry ban list lies in migration to a different country. This may be an option for not only those on the reentry ban list but all interested migrants. Migration to other countries than those in the CIS is already occurring although because stakeholders fear that migration to the Middle East may bring radicalization of youth, regulating this migration may be necessary to avoid negative consequences.

Issues of Female Migration

Some concerns for female migration remain in areas of risks associated with trafficking and exploitation in work. Stakeholders also highlighted the importance of raising awareness of women on the risks of unofficial marriage.[49] Information on reproductive health and remittance management were also identified as needs.

Abandonment of Spouses due to Labor Migration

In mountainous regions, migration for work is a gendered process. Most migrants are male, and women are left behind to bear the responsibility of taking care of children and the elderly, managing household assets, and responding to new challenges. Factors such as social and cultural norms, access to information, and institutional issues act as barriers to adaptation for women (IOM 2019b).

The 2012 Tajikistan Demographic and Health Survey records 21% of all households as female headed, with about 60,000 households made up of single mothers with children. This puts further stress on women, adding economic activities to their traditional role of household work, and care for the children and elderly family members (ADB 2019a).

Men getting married abroad abandoning their family in Tajikistan adversely affects both the immediate and the extended family, the local community, and ultimately the Tajik economy due to the reduction in remittances being sent home but retained in the Russian Federation. Studies by the IOM, UNICEF, and Organization for Security and Co-operation in Europe (OSCE) over the past decade indicate that approximately 30% of wives left behind in Tajikistan end up abandoned by their husbands. This results in the abandoned wives and children being forced to seek help from extended family and friends while they look for other sources of income. These reports also indicate the establishment of a significant number of self-help groups for abandoned wives in all regions from which migrants go abroad. These groups have been developed by a range of NGOs supported by international donors who provide a range of services including micro financing, and micro-small business training including the establishment of cooperatives (ADB 2019a).

To improve the situation of migrant families, it is important to address the negative social aspects of labor migration by empowering women who are left behind and enhancing the protection services offered to them and their children. Some organizations are providing free legal and psychological assistance to these women from migrant families. However, there is not enough training catered to the needs of women. In an interview, the Food and Agricultural Organization (FAO) of the United Nations (UN) also pointed out that most migrants are from rural areas, and there is only one agriculture-related training (in Dangara) among all training centers.

---

[49]   Unofficial marriage, in the former Soviet countries including the Russian Federation, is defined as living together for a long period without registering with the marriage authorities. Often it is referred to as civil marriage. In the former Soviet countries, to date, religious marriages are still considered unofficial if not registered. Official marriage is a marriage that is registered in the office of registration of marriages and births. This authority issues the certificate of birth, marriage, etc. In particular for women, if one does not have the certificate of marriage, her marriage is unofficial and is not entitled to any legal right, such as alimony.

The situation of the left-behind children of migrants requires more careful attention and review. There are cases of school dropouts. The situation is worse when both parents leave and the children are raised by grandparents, who are not capable of looking after teenagers who have money to spend. According to expert interviews, crime has been on the rise among these left-behind teenagers and youth (EUI 2014).

Challenges in the Recruitment Process

There is a need for better institutionalization of recruitment mechanisms so that migrants can more easily access the labor market of destination countries. Currently, labor migration is organized primarily (86%) by migrants' own support networks (JICA 2019). By contrast, according to the Agency of Labor and Employment in 2019, about 2,000 migrants left through recruiting agencies (referred to as migration agencies in Tajikistan), among half a million total labor migrants. Self-regulation of recruitment and employment could be facilitated by a free and easily accessible electronic database of available jobs.

Review of Existing Predeparture and Post-Return Services for Migrant Workers

This section primarily focuses on the predeparture and post-return services for migrant workers by the Government of Tajikistan; however, it does not identify or discuss other types of migrant services provided by the government.

Predeparture and Post-Return Service Needs Identified by Migrant Workers

The great majority of first-time migrants leave without having any detailed knowledge about the situation in the country to which they are traveling. Very few contact the migration centers prior to their departure. As a result, most leave without awareness of the rules and procedures for migrant workers in the Russian Federation, or even having information about potential employers (ADB 2019a).

In an FGD, the migrants stated that "people leaving first time don't come for help, you come to the centers only when you have problems." Asked what they think would have helped them before they left, they answered, "1. language, 2. rights, 3. history and culture, 4. law, 5. how to conduct yourself—in that order." In another FGD, the migrants sequenced their needs in the following order: "1. language, 2. skills, 3. rights, and 4. law and documentation in the Russian Federation." Other recommendations included the following:

- "how to talk to the police and how to deal with the police;"
- "more representatives of MOLME, who can help us deal with legal issues, such as deportation;"
- "we should be given contact details of MOLME representatives in the destination countries;"
- "the government should promote the rights of migrants in the Russian Federation;
- "adjustment in the destination country and after return;"
- "remittance management."

A number of migrants also stated that they would have advised their younger self not to go.

> **"I have been in the Russian Federation for 15 years. Discrimination is the main issue."—Interview with a migrant worker, 4 February 2020.**

Other comments include the lack of information makes migrants, particularly first-time migrants, easy targets for illegal job agents and corrupt bureaucrats. Also, often they lack basic financial competencies, which means they are not good at managing the money they earn while abroad.

In addition to general concerns for the need for job creation in the country for returning migrants, needs for mutual recognition of diplomas were highlighted in the FGDs. University degrees are recognized in the Russian Federation; however, skill-based diplomas are not recognized.[50] One reason identified by the stakeholders is that skills training in Tajikistan is not equivalent to international or Russian standards. Training in the Russian Federation has been modernized. Some migrants commented that this was one of the reasons they do not take training in Tajikistan to improve their skills, but they plan to develop their skills in the Russian Federation. A need for recognition of skills gained abroad was also highlighted by the return migrants and stakeholders.

It should be noted that insufficient services are provided to address the issue of limited job opportunities in the areas that return migrants tend to live. Appropriate labor counseling and support to develop entrepreneurial skills are necessary and would be helpful for returning migrants to find employment in Tajikistan or start their own micro- or small business (ADB 2019a).

Services Provided by the Center for Migrants

Of the four predeparture centers in the country, the Pre-Departure Center for Migrants in Dushanbe is an established center with a staff of 14; the other three centers are poorly staffed and lack basic equipment and facilities (ADB 2019a). Estimates are that 50% of the current staff are young with no training in providing migrant service (ADB-Govt of Tajikistan MOU-SEEP 2019). No centralized training program exists for the staff; they learn through a mentorship program.[51] Stakeholders identified the need for a structured training with reference materials. Training topics should include all migration-related issues, including how to train and interact with migrants. In addition, the need for referral services, for example, legal support through lawyers and trained counselors, was mentioned.

Field research in Tajikistan revealed that the PDO program organized by MOLME's Pre-Departure Centers take the form of consultations instead of a

structured orientation training. They are organized on an ad hoc basis per demand. The predeparture service provided in these centers is limited to 30- to 40-minute talks and provision of some print materials (ADB-Govt of Tajikistan MOU-SEEP 2019). There is no common program of action for PDO, and it is purely based on need. If a group of migrants ask for something, the centers provide. The principal predeparture service offered is a basic introduction to the legislation and regulations applying to labor migrants to the Russian Federation. In addition to the government, a number of NGOs and international organizations offer support; however, only a fraction of the migrants is reached.

The centers offer not only predeparture services but also assistance to returning migrants. The Dushanbe center is servicing significantly more returning migrants than those departing.

The majority of post-return services are provided for the migrants on the reentry ban list of the Russian Federation. With almost 267,324 Tajik migrants in the reentry ban list as of December 2019, Migration Services is understaffed (ADB 2019a) and overwhelmed with the sheer number of reentry ban listees. The major function is to assist the migrants on a case-by-case basis to obtain the removal of the migrants' names from the banned list.

According to an ADB report (2019a), the migration services provided by MOLME are facing a number of limitations, affecting the quality of services:

- The Migration Department's limited capacity and knowledge lead to the great majority of migrants continuing to leave Tajikistan without proper knowledge about the legislation regulating their stay abroad and their rights (and obligations) as migrant workers.
- Most migrants leave without having any officially recognized skills, and for those who have an official certificate issued by the Tajik authorities, these documents are not accepted by the Russian and Kazakh authorities and employers.

---

[50]   Interview with Ismatulloev Ismatullo Ubaydovich, deputy team leader, TRTA, SEEP.
[51]   Quddusov. 2011. Evaluation of Services Provided to Labor Migrants by Dushanbe Pre-Departure Service Center. 10 October.

- The preemployment service centers have no knowledge as to in-demand skills by the Russian labor market and are therefore unable to guide prospective migrants.
- Statistical data on returning migrants are weak as the migration service centers have no system for recording the "clients" they serve.
- The psychosocial problems faced by many migrants banned from returning to the Russian Federation have been widely ignored, as the Migration Service has no expertise in this field.
- Support for reintegrating family or finding work is very limited at the centers due to the lack of trained family and job counselors (ADB-Govt of Tajikistan MOU-SEEP 2019).

The Dushanbe Migration Center has a Russian Language Exam Lab wherein the Russian Migration Federal Service organizes an exam on the Russian language online. Upon completion of the test, migrants are issued a certificate recognized throughout the Russian Federation. The cost of the service is lower in the Dushanbe Center compared to the cost of the test if taken in the Russian Federation. Only accredited agencies can administer the Russian Language exam for migrants.

Since 2014, the number of citizens' contacts to the migration centers has grown significantly, with most of such citizens representing returnees seeking various reintegration services. However, these centers were originally established to provide predeparture services; therefore, they do not have the capacity to provide a full range of reintegration services (Quddusov 2011).

Reintegration of returning migrants remains a serious challenge, both economically and socially. In addition to the limited services provided by MOLME's predeparture centers, a number of NGOs and international organizations, such as IOM, offer support to migrants, particularly those banned from reentry to the Russian Federation. Most support deals with assistance in establishing small local enterprises. Another area of support is assistance in certifying skills acquired while working abroad. A number of training institutions, including adult learning centers (ALCs), are accredited to conduct such tests (recognition of prior learning). However, as mentioned, the

experience from this effort has been mixed due to non-transparent assessment procedures and lack of adequate testing facilities (ADB 2019a).

Digital Information on Migration

In Tajikistan, 6.9 million of the total population of 9.1 million are mobile phone users and 2.95 million are internet users. Compared to nearly half (44%) of the population in Asia and the Pacific, only a third of the Tajik population are internet users.

The National Development Strategy 2030 (NDS 2030) of Tajikistan identifies "low level of implementation of electronic document management system at the state administration bodies and electronic communication of state bodies with citizens and businesses" as a challenge. In some areas relevant to migrants, the NDS 2030 expects the following results:

- "electronic document management system is widely used within the public administration";
- "development of unified electronic database of recipients of social benefits";
- "bridging the digital divide (gap) in different regions, particularly in rural and remote areas."

MOLME is in the process of developing an electronic registration system and database with IOM. However, since registration is not compulsory, many migrants do not register with the government. In meetings with the stakeholders, the importance of data collection and compilation was brought up as a focus area for the government, as lack of detailed and centralized data affects policy and strategy formulation. Additionally, digital information provided on migration services and migration information are not mobile app based but mostly web based.

Migration Service of the Republic of Tajikistan in the Russian Federation has its separate website, which provides information about the site's activity: http://www.tajmigration.ru/. Human Rights Center, in a 2014 report, analyzed the content of the Migration Service website and offered the following observations:

- The website contains information with the address and phone numbers of the organizations in Moscow, as well as contact information (including mobile phones) of the representatives of the Migration Service of Tajikistan in different regions of the Russian Federation.
- The website contains some useful information that could potentially help the migrant in solving legal problems: step-by-step recommendations to migrant workers on registration and legalization of their employment in the Russian Federation (both in Russian and Tajik); links to portals, where migrants from Tajikistan can find a job; and lists and contact details (including mobile phones) of Tajik diaspora and NGOs in different regions of the Russian Federation.
- According to the HRC report, the Migration Service website does not, however, host information about what specific situations migrant workers can approach the service for help and exact legal issues that are within the competence of the organization.

The Employment Service (represented by the Agency of Labor and Employment) has a website containing information about vacancies (www.kor.tj), but it is not updated regularly. What is needed is a Labor Market Information System containing data and analytical information on the labor market situation, labor market dynamics, opportunities for training, ranking professions and characteristics of professions, as well as information on how to choose a profession and career opportunities (ADB 2019a).

Labor Migration Challenges during and after the COVID-19 Pandemic

According to the World Health Organization (WHO), as of 10 August 2020, 25,602,665 confirmed COVID-19 cases and 852,758 deaths have been reported worldwide.[52] The WHO announcement of the pandemic phase on 11 March caused a sharp increase in movement restrictions both at international and local levels, including border closures and nationwide quarantines.[53] Protecting lives and allowing health care systems to cope have required isolation, lockdowns, and widespread closures to slow the spread of the virus.[54] With the health crisis having a severe impact on economic activities, the International Monetary Fund (IMF) projects the global economy to contract 3% in 2020 and by 4.4% in Europe and Central Asia (IMF 2020). Notably, the high dependence on remittances from the Russian Federation is likely to increase the impact of negative external shocks on the Central Asian economies of the Kyrgyz Republic, Tajikistan, and Uzbekistan (KNOMAD 2020).

One of the hardest-hit sectors will be construction. Remittances sent home by millions of expatriate workers in the Russian Federation—coming primarily from construction-sector employment—will be greatly affected.

The following situations are expected to arise:

- Migrants have been stranded when the first restrictions were imposed and will be stranded again if nations are forced to close the border to control the spread of the virus. When travel restrictions were imposed in Central Asia, hundreds of migrant workers from Central Asian countries were stranded at various airports after the Russian Federation and other neighboring countries closed borders and grounded flights to the Kyrgyz Republic, Tajikistan, and Uzbekistan, forcing them to camp out at the terminals for weeks until the issue was resolved by their respective governments (KNOMAD 2020). Migrants were forced to stay at various border points, crowded airports, and train stations, unable to self-quarantine. Steps should be undertaken now to avoid the repetition of similar situations when labor migration opens up again.
- Vulnerable group of migrants will be in detention centers and labor camps or dormitories, where social distancing to reduce the risk of contagion is not possible.

---

[52]   Data as received by WHO from national authorities by 3.56 pm CEST, 2 September 2020. https://covid19.who.int/.
[53]   IOM. 2020. *IOM Global Strategic Preparedness and Response Plan: Coronavirus Disease 2019* (February–December 2020). 15 April.
[54]   IMF. 2020. *World Economic Outlook.* Chapter 1, Washington, DC, April.

- The stock of international migrants will not decrease immediately. Travel restrictions and disruption and absence of transport service will force many migrant workers to remain in the destination countries regardless of whether they are employed. After travel restrictions are lifted, a large number of migrants are expected to travel back to their home countries, increasing the chances of the virus spreading. Safe travel for these migrants needs to be considered as well.
- Migrants remaining in destination countries are in a vulnerable position. Because migrants primarily live in overcrowded facilities in cities, they are more vulnerable to COVID-19. The government, through its embassies, can play a role in reducing the vulnerability of its migrants by providing necessary support, coordiantion with international organizations, CSOs, NGOs, and migrant associations.
- The crisis could also aggravate xenophobic, discriminatory treatment of migrants (KNOMAD 2020).
- Migrant workers—more than native-born workers—tend to be vulnerable to the loss of employment and wages during an economic crisis in their host country (KNOMAD 2020). According to IOM, migrants will remain among the most vulnerable to the loss of economic opportunities, eviction, and homelessness, as well as stigmatization and exclusion from essential services.[55] "When migrants and displaced communities are excluded from national response plans and services, particularly health care, everyone is at greater risk."[56]
- In most destination countries, migrants lack access to public health care services. However, in this situation, control of COVID-19 cases in any country will depend on the health of not only its citizens but also its migrant population.
- According to the KNOMAD Migration and Development Brief on the COVID-19 crisis, the crisis has created additional challenges in sectors in the destination countries that depend on the availability of migrant workers. The crisis has disproportionately impacted food and hospitality, retail and wholesale, tourism and transport, and manufacturing sectors.
- Accessing brick-and-mortar remittance service providers has become difficult. Although many migrants are sending remittances digitally, poor and irregular migrants have low or no access to such instruments. Many Tajik migrant families in rural areas also lack access to online facilities to receive remittances. This might increase reliance on informal money transfers.

The Government of Tajikistan needs to devise strategies for the protection of migrant workers—regardless of their migration and legal status, be it returned migrants, stranded migrants, or those working in destination countries, newly or re-migrating. To safeguard the livelihood of migrants and their families, the government needs to work in close cooperation with the destination country governments and other development partners to devise strategies of safe migration options during and after the pandemic and ensure the continued inflow of remittances that are vital in meeting the daily needs of the recipient families.

MOLME in consultation with stakeholders has developed the plan. Addressing the Impact of COVID-19 on the Labour Market and Migration in the Republic of Tajikistan (3 June 2020) in which various actions to support Tajik labor migrants abroad and labor migrants in Tajikistan who are unable to migrate are outlined. It will be critical that NGOs and aid agencies support the ministry in its efforts.

---

55 UN News. 2020. *Migrants Among Most Vulnerable, As IOM Ramps Up Coronavirus Response Worldwide.* 15 April. https://news.un.org/en/story/2020/04/1061842?fbclid=IwAR3qzPMLOel4AiioRocd-iATxeWy9_1Fg-iy47GSvwItY-ozMMY0bp4iAsE (accessed on 20 April 2020).

56 IOM Director General Vitorino. Quoted in UN News. 2020.

Good Practices: Predeparture and Post-Return Services

Introduction

Migrant services are systems developed by the governments and nongovernment actors to meet migrants' needs and manage migration. Migrant services or migration services are terms that are often used synonymously. These services—which can be for individual migrants' needs at all stages of migration or for the government to manage migration—are developed to meet the needs of migrants and their families. Many labor-origin countries maintain a welfare fund, dedicated to developing and maintaining migrant services.

For the purpose of this study, some good practices of predeparture and post-return services carried out by five selected labor-origin countries as examples of successful migration services (Bangladesh, Indonesia, Nepal, the Philippines, and Sri Lanka) in Asia are discussed in this chapter. Although these are examples from Asia, the practices are relevant to Central Asia. Also included in this section are some examples of projects from Tajikistan.

Stages of Migration and Needs of Migrant Workers

Migration does not occur in discrete steps; it is instead an ongoing process with various stages (predeparture, post-arrival, and return and reintegration), and each stage has its own vulnerabilities and strategies for intervention (Table 3).[57]

Table 3: General Needs of Migrants in Different Stages of Migration

Stage of Migration	Information Need
Predeparture	Knowledge of costs, benefits, risks associated with migration.
	Information on job availability, conditions of contract and placement, financial resources to meet migration expenses, assistance in making domestic arrangements during their absence, and preparing for work overseas, including psychological preparedness for safe migration.
	Standards and certification of required skills.
	Knowledge of culture, expected attitudes, and behavior at destination.
Post-arrival	Information on access to decent working conditions and humane treatment and support (psychosocial, legal), in the event of problems in destination countries.
	Information and support in remitting income and maintaining communications with their families at home.
Return and reintegration	Development of financial stability through proper investment of their earnings.
	Access to investments that would generate maximum income, and access to credit, technical services, marketing, and other facilities for migrant workers wishing to create self-employment activities.
	Counseling in dealing with intra-family difficulties and with reintegration into the community.

Source: IOM. 2005a. *Labor Migration in Asia: Protection of Migrant Workers, Support Services and Enhancing Development Benefits.* Geneva.

Reintegration is often followed by re-migration, thus completing the cycle of migration (Figure 3).

---

[57] Masud. 2005. Pre-Departure Orientation Programme: Study of Good Practices in Asia—A Comparative Study of Bangladesh, the Philippines and Sri Lanka. In *Labour Migration in Asia: Protection of Migrant Workers, Support Services and Enhancing Development Benefits.* Geneva: International Organization for Migration.

Figure 3:   Migration Cycle

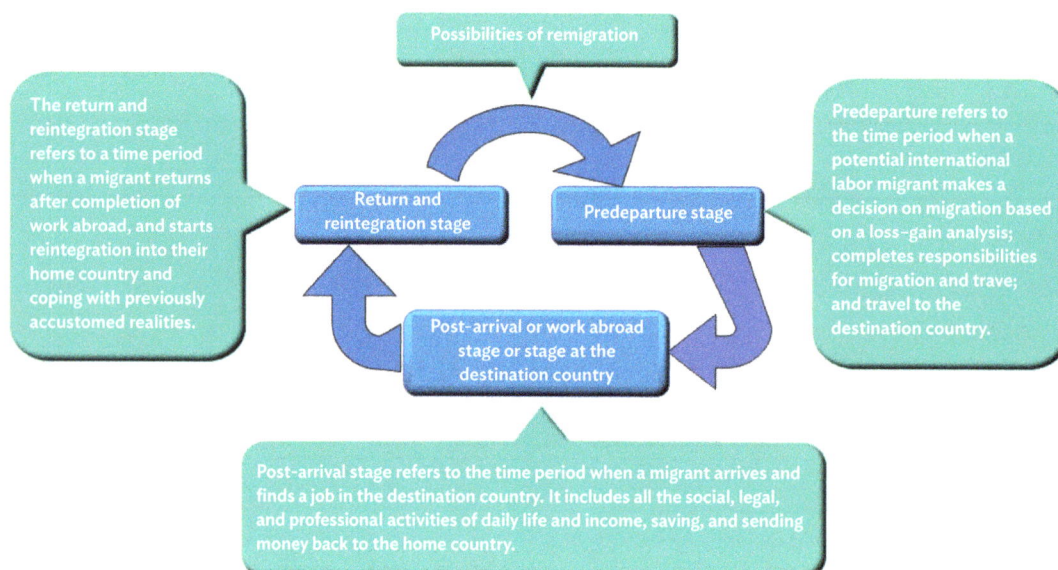

Source: Migration cycle has been first detailed in CARAM Asia's training program on HIV/AIDS and mobility in 2004. The figure is adapted by the authors for this report.

As each stage is linked to the other, it is important to address all relevant issues at different stages. Migration is a cycle, starting in the community, going into the predeparture stage, then the journey, post-arrival, life abroad, the return home, and finally reintegration into the local community (Masud 2005).

In addition to reducing the vulnerabilities of the migrant, maintaining the security of the family members is an important issue for the overall success of migration. Migrant services target all stages of migration as well as families left behind, to reduce vulnerabilities and provide social protection.

International Migration at a Glance: Selected Countries in South and Southeast Asia

The following sections discuss some good practices from five selected labor-origin countries. A number of countries in the South and Southeast Asia regions have been providing migrant services for years. In both regions, short-term labor migration increased exponentially in the 1970s after the oil boom in the Middle East, with the Middle East being the major country of destination. However, over the years, destinations have diversified to include Southeast Asia

(as destination as well as origin), East Asia, Western Europe, and North America. Some notable programs in the two regions, particularly in the area of predeparture orientation seminar (PDOS), are implemented by Bangladesh, Indonesia, Nepal, the Philippines, and Sri Lanka. These countries all provide PDOS as a first step in protecting workers, in addition to other services.

Although the history and pattern of migration are different in each country, all countries have institutionalized international migration as a tool for economic development. Remittances earned through migration are a major source of foreign currency and a significant part of the GDP (see Table 4).

Among the five countries, the Philippines has the most diversity in destination; however, to date, the Middle East remains the major destination for all five countries. The Philippines also ratified all international conventions to protect its workers.

Table 4:   International Migration at a Glance:
Selected Countries in South and Southeast Asia

	Bangladesh	Indonesia	Nepal	Philippines	Sri Lanka
Total population (2018) (million)[a]	164.6	265.0	29.1	106.6	21.7
International migrants (outflow/year) (000s)[b]	700.16 (2019)	264.09 (2018)	382.87[e]	2,299 (2018)	263.31 (2017)
Male international migrants, % of total migrants (outflow/year)	85 (2019)	32 (2018)	94.74 (2016-17)	44.15 (2018)	66 (2017)
Female international migrants, female % of total migrants (outflow/year)	15 (2019)	68 (2018)	5.26 (2016-17)	55.85 (2018)	34 (2017)
Remittance inflows, January to October 2019 ($ million)[cd]	17,539	11,679	8,643	35,071	7,681
Remittance, as a percentage of GDP in 2019[c]	5	1.1	29.9	9.8	9.1

[a] Source of population data: Asian Development Bank.

Bangladesh
https://data.adb.org/dataset/bangladesh-key-indicators

Indonesia
https://data.adb.org/dataset/indonesia-key-indicators

Nepal
https://data.adb.org/dataset/nepal-key-indicators

The Philippines
https://data.adb.org/dataset/philippines-key-indicators

Sri Lanka
https://data.adb.org/dataset/sri-lanka-key-indicators)

[b] Data reflect documented migrants only

[c] The World Bank; Migration and Remittances Data; Annual Remittances Data https://www.worldbank.org/en/topic/migrationremittancesdiasporaissues/brief/migration-remittances-data

[d] Remittance sent by total migrant stock over 10 months

[e] Excludes migration data to India

Sources of migrant data:

Bangladesh: Bureau of Manpower, Employment and Training (BMET); Overseas Employment in 2019 http://www.old.bmet.gov.bd/BMET/viewStatReport.action?reportnumber=34; Overseas Employment of Female workers in 2019 http://www.old.bmet.gov.bd/BMET/viewStatReport.action?reportnumber=29

Indonesia: National Board for the Placement and Protection of Indonesian Overseas Workers (BNP2TKI); Presentation at "Strengthening the Collection and Use of International Migration Data in the Context of the 2030 Agenda for Sustainable Development," Bangkok, 5–8 February 2019. https://www.unescap.org/sites/default/files/3%20Session%207%20Country%20presentation%20Indonesia.pdf

Nepal: Ministry of Labor and Employment, Government of Nepal; *Labor Migration for Employment: A Status Report for Nepal – 2015-16–2016-17*; 2018 https://asiafoundation.org/wp-content/uploads/2018/05/Nepal-Labor-Migration-status-report-2015-16-to-2016-17.pdf

Philippines: Philippine Statistics Authority. *2018 Survey on Overseas Filipinos,* Table 1.1: Distribution of Overseas Filipino Workers 2018.

Sri Lanka: Sri Lanka Bureau of Foreign Employment. *Annual Statistical Report of Foreign Employment 2017.* http://www.slbfe.lk/file.php?FID=487

Good Practices: Predeparture Services

Predeparture services begin with awareness raising among potential migrants on the risks and benefits of migration. At the pre-decision stage, awareness can be well as targeted preemployment orientation seminars (PEOSs). Predeparture services can be provided by the government, CSOs, or private sectors. Some of these services include the following:

A. Mass awareness-raising campaigns: At the pre-decision-making stage, awareness campaigns represent an important step in promoting safe, orderly, and regular migration. Potential migrants are provided with a wide range of information, such as the cost benefits of migration, methods of fraudulent practices, fair recruitment practices, and overseas employment opportunities. Mass awareness raising can be delivered through local government-level units, technical and vocational training centers, religious leaders, grassroots-level organizations, and media. The mode of awareness raising could be advertisements, drama, focused programs for migrants on TV and radio, printed materials, online information dissemination, rallies, popular theatre shows, meeting at the village level, and so forth.

B. Preemployment orientation seminars: PEOS is planned out at the pre-decision-making stage and can be provided by governments and CSOs. Although predeparture briefing is mandatory in the five selected countries, it comes at the last moment for many migrant workers, when they have already paid the informal migration agents and therefore are unwilling to step back even if they feel that the endeavor might be risky. The objective of a PEOS program is to enhance the awareness of the potential migrants on the realities of migration, discuss how to avoid falling prey to traffickers and fraudulent practices of migration, and to empower the potential migrants to make a decision that considers the costs and the benefits.

C. Skills training: Skill enhances the possibilities of better-paid jobs for migrant workers. Technical and

Box 1:   Preemployment Orientation Seminars in the Philippines

The Philippine Overseas Employment Administration (POEA) provides comprehensive PEOS that will discuss topics such as prevention of illegal recruitment and gender sensitivity. It is part of the intensified programme of the government against illegal recruitment activities. PEOS is conducted to provide information on labor and employment conditions, migration realities and other facts on overseas employment, and to adequately prepare participants into making informed and intelligent decisions about overseas employment. POEA has conducted PEOS in schools, tapped local government units through the Public Employment Service Offices, conducted PEOS in regions through Department of Labor and Employment regional offices, and developed country-specific information materials for PEOS.

Source: International Labour Organization. 2014. *Assessment of the Existing Services for Skilled Migrant Workers in the Philippines.* Manila.

vocational training in particular enhances the skills of potential migrants.

According to an ILO Policy Brief (2018),[58] due to tighter restrictions on unskilled labor migration in many countries of destination, low-skilled individuals are also more likely to migrate irregularly. As undocumented migrants, they are especially vulnerable to exploitation since they fear job loss, incarceration, and deportation. Therefore, they tend to work in the informal economy, where they lack access to social and legal protection. Moreover, they are likely to work in sectors or occupations that are more dangerous than others, often serving as the labor force that fills the "3-D" (dirty, difficult, dangerous) jobs. For origin countries of labor migrants, enhancing skills not only helps migrants achieve better employment opportunities but also protects their rights.

Another important area in skill development is language. Developing language skills is as necessary as work-related skills. Multiple studies identify language skills as a necessary component of predeparture training. Better language proficiency means better job opportunities. In addition to economic gain, language skills influence non-economic outcomes, such as

---

[58]   ILO. 2018. *Skills for Migration and Employment.* Policy Brief. Skills for Employment.

better social integration in the host country, ability to communicate with authorities, health care and other services of the destination countries, increased social network, among other benefits. Migrants often need to learn the language at the destination country, making the initial contact and integration (economic, social, and psychosocial) difficult. Many labor-origin countries provide destination country- and in some cases skill-specific language training programs.

D. Finding employment: In Tajikistan, an informal recruitment method prevails. The role of the state and the private sector is negligible when it comes to overseas employment. However, many countries find it difficult to control private recruitment agencies and sub-agents. Some employment is organized under G2G (government to government) agreements through bilateral agreements and memoranda of understanding (MOUs).

> ### Box 2:   Employment Permit System in the Republic of Korea
>
> The Republic of Korea's Employment Permit System (EPS), established in 2004, is perhaps the clearest example of a government-to-government recruitment regime that has replaced private recruitment agencies with public employment services. The EPS operates through the conclusion of memoranda of understanding between the Republic of Korea and countries of origin. To date, 15 memoranda of understanding have been signed under the program. There is no space for private actors in the EPS recruitment process.
>
> Source: Open Working Group on Labor Migration and Recruitment. n.d. Policy Brief 3. *Government-to-Government Recruitment Benefits & Drawbacks.*

However, not all G2G agreements exclude private recruiting agency involvement as the Republic of Korea.

E. Predeparture orientation seminar: PDOS can impart practical knowledge about migrants' future living and working environment and cover such topics as basic language skills, financial management, health counseling, and human rights awareness. The overall objective is to equip departing migrants with reliable and accurate information regarding their employment and life abroad, return, and reintegration; protect migrant workers from potential abusive employment practices in the country of destination; and enhance the gains that can be made in orderly labor migration through a short course.[59]

PDO courses are often targeted to labor migrants who have secured an employment contract. These courses have expanded its focus from knowledge, skills, and attitudes needed to facilitate their integration into destination countries to skills training, language training, preemployment training, counseling, and much more. Courses may be tailored to specific demographics and populations (OSCE, IOM, and ILO 2006).

Countries have established PDO programs as an integral tool for the protection of migrant workers. Although PDOS is merely one component of a successful model for protecting migrants and should be complementary to pre-decision-making programs, support at destination countries, and post-return services, its importance cannot be underscored. Existing PDO programs are extensively discussed in Predeparture Orientation Seminars.

F. Migration loan: Migration loans are provided to the vulnerable population to reach their migration goals. Loans can be provided by government banks, private banks, or microfinance institutes. Some households use microcredit as an advance on expected remittances from family members abroad; others use loans to finance the costs of migration.[60]

G. Services for assisting in acquiring visas, contracts, and medical checkups and checking contracts. The governments are the primary providers of these services for migrant workers leaving under the G2G schemes. In case of migration through recruiting agencies, migrant workers can check with the government (for example, the Philippines) as to

---

59   OSCE, IOM, and ILO. 2006. *Handbook on Establishing Effective Labour Migration Policies in Countries of Origin and Destination.* Helsinki.

60   MPI. 2013. *The Growing Linkages Between Migration and Microfinance.* Migration Information Source. 13 June. https://www.migrationpolicy.org/article/growing-linkages-between-migration-and-microfinance.

whether the recruiting agency they are dealing with is legal.

Predeparture Orientation Seminars

For many migrant workers, PDO is where they first glean a realistic sight into their potential life in destination countries, the challenges they might face, and how to meet those challenges. It is also the home government's first step in preparing migrant workers for departure through training and educational programs. Predeparture information programs are premised on two concepts: (1) that the protection of migrants begins at home and (2) that information builds a foundation for migrant empowerment and protection.[61]

To ensure that migration is beneficial to the migrant worker and his or her family, PDOS is an important component of the whole cycle of migration and is designed to help migrants: (i) make a knowledge-based decision to migrate, (ii) reduce their vulnerability, (iii) match skills with employer demand, (iv) ease the transition into the country of destination, (v) ease the return and reintegration back into the economy and society of the home country, and (vi) maximize benefits from overseas employment in each stage of migration. Therefore, PDOS provides information, skill, method, and specific documents to departing migrant for all these three stages (predeparture, post-arrival, and post-return) for both the migrant and his or her family.

The following are the main potential benefits of the services:

- A decision to migrate that is knowledge based will avoid the costs associated with suffering the consequences of a wrong decision and reduce the vulnerabilities of the migrants.
- The combination of technical training—including on-the-job training, life skills training, language training, and job guidance—will generate the benefit of obtaining better paid jobs more quickly in the host country.

- Awareness of opportunities and risks will generate for the departing migrants a maximized benefit of overseas work and avoidance of costs associated with preventable negative incidents during the entire migration process (ADB 2019a).
- Assistance after return from overseas will produce the benefit of speedy reintegration of the migrants into society and into the labor market with earnings that will be made soon after return (ADB 2019a).

The individual services listed here cannot be calculated separately. The benefits of technical training, which usually can be evaluated by using earnings after graduation, cannot be dissociated from the predeparture program (ADB 2019a). Successful programs are already being carried out by some countries in Asia. Some good practices from selected countries are discussed in the following subsection.

Predeparture Orientation Seminars in South and Southeast Asia Regions

Each country designs its PDO programs based on its migration scenario and migrant profile. If necessary and if budget allows, PDO seminars may be different based on profession as well as destination (Table 5). Each country's PDO has its pros and cons.

Discussions of some of the government agencies relevant to migration management and mechanism of imparting PDOS in the five selected countries follow:

Bangladesh: The Ministry of Expatriates' Welfare and Overseas Employment is entrusted to protect the rights and the interest of migrants in the host country, as well as in Bangladesh when they return or are about to leave. The Bureau of Manpower Employment and Training (BMET) has been responsible for formal international migration since 1976. BMET is an autonomous body and the implementing agency of the Ministry of Expatriates' Welfare and Overseas Employment as well as the Ministry of Labor. Overseas Employment and Migrant Act 2013 is the principal legal instrument in managing migration.

---

[61]   IOM. 2012. *Strengthening Pre-departure Orientation Programs in Indonesia, Nepal and the Philippines.* Issue in Brief. Issue No. 5. Bangkok.

Table 5: Predeparture Information Program of Selected Countries in South and Southeast Asia at a Glance

	Bangladesh	Indonesia	Nepal	Philippines	Sri Lanka
Name of predeparture program	Predeparture Briefing	Predeparture Briefing (PAP)	Predeparture Orientation Training	Predeparture Orientation Seminar (PDOS)	Predeparture Orientation
Launched in	1990	2003	2004	1983	1996[a]
Initiated by	BMET	Recruitment agencies; migrant workers pay	Not known	NGOs; migrant workers	SLBFE
Implementing agency	BMET	BNP2TKI	FEPB	OWWA (since 2003; previously POEA)	SLBFE
Provider(s)	TTC (70) since 2017 under BMET	BNP2TKI, BP3TKI (in 16 provinces)	Private institutions (118)	OWWA, POEA, NGOs (for vulnerable workers), recruitment agencies (58), industry associations	SLBFE
Fees	$2.35 (24 hour) $7.00 (for FMDW)	None	NR 700 ($10); reimbursable for women	Government—none; others—PHP 100 ($2.30)	None
Registration	Mandatory	Not known	Not known	Mandatory	Mandatory
PDO	Mandatory	Mandatory	Mandatory	Mandatory	Mandatory
Length of program	24 hours (since 2017 at the TTCs) and 8 hours at BMET for general migrants; and 30 days for FMDW	8 hours	12.5 hours for women; 11.5 hours for men	6 hours	Half-day

[a] PDOS was made compulsory in 1996; no information is available as to when PDO programs began.

BMET = Bureau of Manpower, Employment and Training, BNP2TKI = National Board for the Placement and Protection of Indonesian Overseas Workers, BP3TKI = Agency for the Service, Placement and Protection of Indonesian Overseas Workers, FEPB = Foreign Employment Promotion Board, FMDW = Female Migrant Domestic Workers, OWWA = Overseas Workers Welfare Administration, NGO = nongovernmental organization, POEA = Philippine Overseas Employment Administration, SLBFE = Sri Lanka Bureau of Foreign Employment, TTC = Technical Training Center.

Source: Partially (Indonesia, Nepal, and the Philippines) adapted from IOM. 2012. *Strengthening Pre-Departure Orientation Programs in Indonesia, Nepal and the Philippines*. Issue in Brief. Issue No. 5. Bangkok. Information source: Bangladesh (BMET) and Sri Lanka (SLBFE). Updated from Nepal (FEPB), the Philippines (OWWA) websites.

BIMT (Bangladesh Institute of Marine Technology), which conducts skills training.[62] PDO is part of skills training in TTCs. In addition to the government curricula, NGOs and migrant associations take extra sessions with the migrant workers on safe migration.

The government also identified inadequate knowledge of language as a deterrent for foreign employment and established an English Language Laboratory at their Dhaka training center to offer language training for two categories of overseas job seekers: nurses and hotel workers. Language training has now expanded to include Arabic, Japanese, and Korean and is administered by the TTCs for different categories of job seekers.

For skilled migrants, Bangladesh Overseas Employment & Services Limited (BOESL)[63] organizes its own preflight briefing. The 2-hour briefing is held 3–4 days before departure. The program includes lectures on the rules, regulations, and traditional background of the country of employment, local customs and guidelines for personal conduct, and workers' obligations under the destination country's local labor laws.

Indonesia: The deployment and protection of Indonesian labor migrants currently involves the participation of at least 13 government institutions including, among other things, the Ministry of Manpower and Transmigration; National Board for the Placement and Protection of Indonesian Overseas Workers (BNP2TKI); the Ministry of Foreign Affairs; the Ministry of Social Affairs; the Coordinating Ministry of Economic Affairs; the Coordinating Ministry of People's Welfare; the Ministry of Health; the Ministry of Communication; the Ministry of Home Affairs; the Directorate General of Immigration; the Indonesian National Police; and the National Body for Professional Certification and the Professional Certification Institute. In addition, the Agency for

the Service, Placement and Protection of Indonesian Overseas Workers (BP3TKI) is responsible for implementation in the provinces.[64]

The Migrant Worker Placement and Protection Law of 2004 states that all migrant workers must complete what is known as the Final Pre-Departure Briefing, or Pembekalan Akhir Pemberangkatan (PAP), which is offered to migrant workers free of charge. Attendance became mandatory in 2003. BNP2TKI, which manages the predeparture briefing, hires some 200 instructors, usually government personnel or retirees. In Jabodetabek (Greater Jakarta) the briefings are usually offered daily in two venues, Cawang and Bekasi (IOM 2012).

Similar briefings are offered in 16 provinces that are major sending areas and are coordinated by BP3TKI, which is a provincial branch established by BNP2TKI in these provinces. This arrangement enables the government to manage and implement the program without having to deal with other entities. The predeparture briefing is offered for free, which is guaranteed by a regulation (IOM 2012).

Nepal: The Ministry of Labor and Employment takes the lead in the formulation, implementation, coordination, monitoring. and evaluation of policies, plans, and programs related to labor and employment as per the Allocation of Business Rules, 2012. Within the Ministry, all matters relating to foreign employment are administered by the Foreign Employment and International Labor Relations Division. The Foreign Employment Promotion Board (FEPB) was established according to section 38 of the Foreign Employment Act and is chaired by the Minister of Labor and Employment. Its main responsibilities are the promotional activities for foreign employment and to ensure the social protection and welfare of migrant workers.[65]

---

[62] Interview with Nurul Islam, director (retired), BMET, 24 January 2020.

[63] Alongside the private sector recruiting agencies, state-owned enterprise (BOESL) is established for recruiting and placing skilled personnel for overseas employment, established by the Government of Bangladesh in 1984. Although BOESL is government-owned, it is a fully autonomous organization and runs commercially to fulfil overseas requirements in skilled manpower.

[64] IOM. 2012. and IOM. 2010b. *Labor Migration from Indonesia: An Overview of Indonesian Migration to Selected Destinations in Asia and the Middle East.* Jakarta.

[65] IOM. 2012 and Government of Nepal. 2016. *Labor Migration for Employment—A Status Report for Nepal: 2014/2015.* Katmandu.

The implementation of PDO is exclusively in the hands of accredited recruitment agencies. The agencies charge NR700 (about $10) for the orientation session. In this configuration, FEPB functions mostly as manager and overseer. The program, known as predeparture orientation, was made mandatory for departing migrant workers in 2004. Chapter 6 of the Foreign Employment Regulation 2064 (2008), deals with provisions related to training. Repatriation of earnings made abroad to Nepal in a simple, easy and safe manner. The FEPB is charged with (i) registering institutions to provide foreign employment orientation training, (ii) developing and approving the curriculum, and (iii) monitoring orientation training. The actual implementation is entirely in the hands of accredited recruitment agencies. There are 50 orientation centers that are licensed to conduct the 2-day predeparture orientation—a total of 12.5 hours and 11.5 hours of instruction for female and male migrants, respectively. Male migrants pay NR700 (about $10) for the orientation, while female migrants are reimbursed by the migrant resource center.

The Philippines: The Philippines' legal framework regarding emigration is contained in Republic Act No. 8042, (the Migrant Workers and Overseas Filipinos Act of 1995). The principal ministries and administrative bodies responsible for labor emigration include the Department of Foreign Affairs, Department of Labor and Employment (DOLE) and its Philippine Overseas Employment Administration (POEA), and Overseas Workers Welfare Administration (OWWA) (Masud 2005).

Predeparture orientation seminars and registration are mandatory for migrants, which is a requirement for an exit permit. The Philippines has developed a multi-stakeholder predeparture orientation program, with the government (OWWA and POEA), civil society, and the private sector as implementers. To ensure that the curriculum emphasizes the protection of migrants, the responsibility for providing PDOS to domestic workers and entertainers was given to NGOs in 1992. Since then, the private sector has ceased to

be the sole provider of PDOS for agency hires (IOM 2012). However, the PDOS program provided by the private sector still covers the largest share of departing overseas Filipino workers (OFWs) (IOM 2012). Presently, the program is conducted by OWWA and POEA and 260 accredited private sector and NGO providers.

All PDOS providers must use the government-prescribed standard syllabus and receive regular updates and advisory notices on policies or relevant developments in host countries. According to an IOM Brief (2012), the current curriculum and manual were developed for OWWA by the Development Academy of the Philippines in 2008, with contributions and inputs from PDOS providers as well as former OFWs and OWWA officers. To ensure that vital information is conveyed to participants across all types of providers, in 2009, OWWA developed a discussion outline. OWWA regularly sends advisories and important information that would benefit migrants. However, the curriculum has remained largely unchanged over the years, with the exception of the addition of "health and safety" and "financial literacy" as topics.

Some PDOs specialize in specific countries. Other orientation programs specialize on specific occupations; an example is the Pre-Decision Booklet on Labor Migration for Health Workers,[66] which provides advice in the process of making the decision to work overseas.

While the PDOS program provided by POEA and OWWA is free (likewise with the Comprehensive Pre-Departure Education Program (CPDEP), nongovernment providers charge PHP100 (approximately $2.30), which is supposed to be shouldered by the agencies (IOM 2012).

Since 1983, the PDOS program in the Philippines has expanded and been supplemented by two other information programs: the PEOS, which precedes PDOS; and the post-arrival orientation seminar (PAOS), which is a follow-up to PDOS and takes

---

[66]   Produced for the Philippines by PSI, Public Services International in France. https://www.ilo.org/wcmsp5/groups/public/---asia/---ro-bangkok/---ilo. - cited in ADB. 2019a.

place in the migrant's destination country. Unlike PDOS, the two programs are not mandatory, and their implementation is less standardized (IOM 2012).

Sri Lanka: The Sri Lanka Bureau of Foreign Employment (SLBFE) is the responsible agency for managing labor migration. SLBFE was established by an Act of Parliament in 1985 as a self-financed public corporation to provide for the systematic regulation of the process of migration and to protect workers and provide for their welfare and their families. A ministerial advisory committee provides policy guidelines to SLBFE (Masud 2005).

Both premigration registration and predeparture orientation are mandatory in Sri Lanka. Registration and mandatory attendance at PDOS entitle the registrant to free insurance coverage and payment of embarkation tax and welfare benefits, such as access to loans from state banks at subsidized interest rates and scholarships for children. PDOS offers one course for the Middle East (120 hours or 12 days of residential training) and for other countries (210 hours or 22 days of residential training) for domestic workers. Training programs are free of charge and are financed from the SLBFE's Welfare Fund. SLBFE operates training centers (17 in 2020) and others (9 in 2003) are operated by accredited employment agencies and NGOs.[67]

All the countries have the following general contents[68] for the PDO seminars:

- Process of migration (medical tests, certification, and documentation) and work contracts
- Immigration and flight procedures
- Working conditions, regulations and laws, culture, and customs of destination countries
- Code of conduct
- Workplace safety
- How-to information about availing of embassy support at destination countries, insurance claim, legal aid, and so forth.
- Remittance transfer

- Health tips (mental and psychological issues, HIV/AIDS, communicable diseases, and sexual and reproductive health)
- Return and reintegration challenges (in some countries to a lesser extent)

Some countries also cover language of the destination country and provide language booklets; some also provide migrants with destination country-specific booklets (for example, Bangladesh and the Philippines) and some provide occupation-specific booklets (for example, for domestic workers).

Lessons Learned on PDOS

Based on the experiences of the five labor-origin countries on PDOS, some good practices and challenges of PDO seminars follow:[69]

Good Practices: The PDO programs developed in the five countries have not always been what they are today. Change was effected with the evolving needs of migrants and changes in migration patterns. Several good practices, which are potentially replicable, include the following:

In program design and management:

- Encouraging predeparture registration and orientation: Registration enables certain advantages for the migrants, for example, insurance, subsidized loans, scholarship, predeparture and post-return loans from government banks, and so forth. It encourages migrant workers to register and opt for documented migration (Masud 2005). In addition, registration also helps the government to collect data on migrants.
- Decentralized predeparture orientation: A geographically decentralized predeparture program helps migrants avail of the information easily (IOM 2012) and involves local governments as partners in PDOS.
- Supplementing predeparture orientations or briefings with other information programs: The PEOS covers decision-making in general,

---

[67]   Sri Lanka Bureau of Foreign Employment (SLBFE). Website: http://www.slbfe.lk/ and Ali. 2005.
[68]   Masud. 2005; IOM. 2012; SLBFE website; and BMET.
[69]   Partially adapted from IOM. 2012 and Ali. 2005.

the process of legal application for overseas employment job opportunities, and the risks of illegal recruitment. This course is designed to be completed before migrants attend PDOS. The PAOS takes place at embassies and consulates. The governments, UN agencies, NGOs, and migrant associations organize awareness-raising programs through mass media as well as community-based orientation programs. These programs provide aspiring migrants with a realistic overview of overseas employment.

- Greater involvement from media infrastructure: Coverage in the media, newspaper, radio, and television suggest that migration is an integral part of life, and the programs also cover a significant number of challenges.

- Involvement of private sector, international organizations, and NGOs: Involving NGOs and other stakeholders helps in decentralization and expansion across the national territory, thereby providing access to a greater number of migrants.

- Developing curricula and supporting activities with destination countries: Key priority messages need to be identified in close consultation with receiving countries and must take into consideration the cultural, linguistic, and socioeconomic challenges that specific groups may encounter upon arrival (IOM n.d.).

- Linking predeparture and post-arrival activities, recognizing the transitional continuum.

- Maximize training accessibility: When planning and budgeting for training, attention must be given to the various needs of the clients, taking into account their age, education, literacy and/or language level, history of persecution, exposure to modern living, and so forth. Programs may provide childcare and/or a travel cost reimbursement, to those who would otherwise not be able to attend the training.

- Scheduling orientation sessions as close to departure as possible: Orientation sessions should be scheduled as soon as possible, without interfering with the departure process itself. This maximizes the retention of new information and ensures that the new information is as relevant as possible (IOM n.d.).

In migrant training approach and methodology:

- Trainers' training: Successful training programs require trainers qualified in modern training methodology. Flexible and innovative training also needs regular updates of lecturers/trainers' skills and knowledge through refresher courses.

- Up-to-date and innovative curricula for predeparture programs: Migration trends and challenges are ever changing, PDOS must therefore be flexible and sufficiently innovative to accommodate changes in context and regime and in the consequences of migration.

- Develop training that is participatory and learner centric.

- Content of PDOS: The predeparture orientation should address the strategic objective of empowering migrants in their process of migration and employment in destination countries. It should cover all stages of migration as well as possible challenges and well-being of families. PDOS should also offer information on government benefits available to migrants (such as loans, housing, insurance). Some other important issues that should be focused in PDOS are psychosocial issues and gender equality.

- It is equally important to provide an open and secure learning environment in which gender equality is promoted. Most importantly, content of the predeparture should be updated regularly to keep in touch with the ever-changing migration scenario.

- Supporting materials for PDO program: Destination country-specific booklets and foreign language training with a handbook on specific vocabulary for selected destinations should be developed. Handbooks, videos, and any other information should be available digitally.

- Train in migrants' native language.

- Provide support to and build the capacity of consular services and migrant representatives to forge ties with migrants and relevant destination-country government institutions.

- Involve cross-cultural or bicultural trainers.

- Identify what the learners already know and then move to what they want or need to learn.

- Address the needs of not only the individual migrant but also the entire family.

Challenges of PDOS: Challenges remain for PDO programs in the five labor-origin countries, and there is room for improvement. Some of these challenges follow:

- If predeparture orientation program is not supplemented by a pre-decision-making program, it may be too late to provide some of the information.

- It is unclear whether migrants acquire necessary and relevant information from predeparture information programs.

- Predeparture information programs tend to have a one-size-fits-all design: there is an increasing need for country-, skill- and gender-specific programs.

- Different stakeholders can hold irreconcilable views about the division of labor in predeparture information programs. Whereas some believe only the governments, or the NGOs should be solely responsible for imparting PDOS, different countries have developed their own model for success.

- There is a vacuum of reliable migration information beyond urban centers.

- There is a lack of coordination among government agencies and between different levels of government.

Post-Return Services

Introduction

Return and reintegration is a step of the migration cycle; many migrants may settle down in their origin country, whereas some re-migrate. The process of return is often followed by a phase of re-inclusion or reincorporation in the economic and social life in the country of origin, which is commonly referred to as reintegration.[70] Post-return services can begin from the destination country, in particular, for migrants in detention and/or in irregular status, who would need and/or want to return to their origin country. It can include counseling, legal aid, medical aid, psychosocial support, and repatriation assistance.

After - return services may include monetary support (for a limited time period), psychosocial support, legal aid, career guidance, skill recognition services, job placement services, technical and vocational training, entrepreneurship skill development and investment support, family reunification, assistance

in remigration, and so forth. The services developed are catered to different types of migrant needs; for example, monetary support, counseling, and legal aid may be provided for migrants who became victims of trafficking, whereas entrepreneurship skill development may be provided for migrants who do not wish to re-migrate and integrate with their origin country as well as for vulnerable migrants. Some return and reintegration services follow (this is not an exhaustive list; for example, consular services are not discussed):

- return assistance to vulnerable migrants
- reintegration assistance to vulnerable migrants
- legal assistance
- skill recognition, predeparture skills training, and (re)migration for overseas employment
- migration loans for return migrants
- social integration
- financial inclusion in the local economy, through local employment, savings, and investment in financial products; low-interest loans (for investment); grant programs; and entrepreneurship development
- psychosocial assistance for both vulnerable and returned migrants

Some countries have programs on the return of qualified nationals on a temporary or permanent basis, in particular for the professional categories of migrants, to address brain drain.

Some of the services overlap between returned migrants under normal circumstances and vulnerable migrants. Skill recognition can also be part of local economic inclusion as well as remigration. Some of the services provided to return migrants can also be a part of larger economic and social programs by the government, international organizations, and local NGOs.

In addition to services developed, it is equally important to build and enhance capacities and infrastructure (policy, legal, and organization structure), both at local and national levels in the country or origin. Coordination is an essential

---

[70]   IOM. 2018b. *Return and Reintegration: Key Highlights.* Geneva.

prerequisite for successful reintegration programs, both between countries at the international level and between stakeholders within the countries.[71]

"Reintegration can be considered sustainable when returnees have reached levels of economic self-sufficiency, social stability within their communities and psychosocial well-being that allow them to cope with (re)migration drivers. Having achieved sustainable reintegration, returnees are able to make further migration decisions as a matter of choice rather than necessity (IOM 2018b)."

Good Practices

A. Return and Reintegration Assistance to Vulnerable Migrants: Some migrants return due to normal circumstances; however, some return due to strenuous circumstances, such as deteriorating health, accidents, deportation due to irregular migration, and so on. Many face challenges they cannot overcome on their own and need support in reintegrating; the factors that affect an individual's reintegration can be economic, social, and psychosocial. Some existing programs include the following:

i)   return assistance by governments
ii) IOM Assisted Voluntary Return and Reintegration (AVRR)
iii) legal assistance

i) Return assistance by governments: Many governments provide return assistance to vulnerable migrants. A general process for the return of a vulnerable migrant, after medical, psychosocial, and legal assistance has been provided, may be as follows:

• Preparing migrants for return through counseling, providing return-related information, issuing travel documents (where necessary), financial assistance for travel (could be from the government, employer, recruiting agents, or CSOs), and transport assistance arrangement.
• During travel, departure assistance (including travel and miscellaneous allowances), transport (movement coordination, transit assistance, and

escort assistance, where necessary), and medical assistance if required.
• After arrival, reception, inland transport assistance, if necessary.

It must be mentioned that migrants should be aware of options available to them, which may include return information, as well as other options to stay in the destination country.

ii) IOM-Assisted Voluntary Return and Reintegration (AVRR): IOM AVRR programs provide a human rights–based, migrant-friendly, and cost-effective option to migrants whose journey had taken a different route than what was initially expected and who desire or need to return home but lack the means to do so (IOM 2018b).

Beneficiaries of the IOM AVRR programs may include stranded migrants in host or transit countries, irregular migrants, regular migrants, and asylum seekers who decide not to pursue their claims or who are no longer in need of international protection (IOM 2018b). IOM AVRR programs are either available to all migrants in an irregular situation in a particular country or tailored to the particular needs of particular groups, including migrants with specific needs (e.g., trafficked persons).[72]

Each AVRR program consists of three essential elements: predeparture assistance, transportation assistance, and post-arrival assistance.[73] Between 2013 and 2018, 1,048 migrants were returned to Tajikistan under its AVRR program (IOM 2018b).

After return, post-arrival services may include longer-term reintegration assistance to facilitate sustainable returns (e.g., support for vocational training, income-generating activities, and so forth.) (UNHCR 2017).

iii) Legal assistance: Legal assistance is provided at the destination country as required; however, depending on cases, legal assistance may need to be provided after return. Labor-origin countries developed structures to provide legal assistance directly or through a referral system with the NGOs.

71   IOM. 2014b. *Reference Guide: Labor Attaches of Bangladesh.* Dhaka.
72   UNHCR. 2017. *The 10-Point Plan.* Geneva.
73   IOM. 2010a. *Practical Guide on Information Provision on Return and Reintegration in Countries of Origin.* Geneva.

Box 3:   Legal Assistance for Migrant Workers in the Philippines

In the Philippines, relevant government agencies provide legal assistance to migrant workers in times of need, especially during situations where violations happened in destination countries. The anti-illegal recruitment branch of the Philippine Overseas Employment Agency (POEA) provide free legal assistance for the victims. This is in cooperation with the Department of Justice, the Integrated Bar of the Philippines, and other nongovernmental organizations and volunteer groups. According to the 2014 ILO report, a total of about $2 million is to be allotted for the legal assistance fund. The fund shall be used exclusively in provision of legal services to Filipino migrant workers facing charges, or those filing cases against abusive employers. The fund is also used to pay bail bonds and other litigation expenses.

The Commission on Filipinos Overseas (CFO) has developed "global legal assistance and advocacy" (GLADD) with a goal to establish networks of legal experts that will voluntarily assist OFW victims of illegal recruitment and abusive injustices. GLADD programs include "representation in courts and other tribunals, drafting and filing of legal documents, legal counseling, providing a forum for advocacy, and lobbying efforts aimed at advancing the interests of overseas Filipino communities" (Global Legal Assistance and Advocacy 2012).

Source: International Labour Organization. 2014. *Assessment of the Existing Services for Skilled Migrant Workers in the Philippines.* Manila.

B. Skill recognition, predeparture skills training, and remigration for overseas employment: Skill recognition of already-acquired skills is an important part of assisting migrants attain better-paid jobs in the home country or abroad. Predeparture training skill development/recognition and remigration is another area of focus for assisting migrants who wish to re-migrate or for new migrants. See Box 4 for an example of good practice.

C. Loans after return: Loans for skill development, re-migration, and economic inclusion can be offered by the government, private banks, and microfinance institutes.

D. Financial inclusion and social integration: Financial inclusion in the local economy may include local employment, savings, and investment in financial

Box 4:   Case Study on BDO Academy in Tajikistan

BDO Academy administers a program wherein potential and return migrants are trained with financial assistance from the ADB Market-Responsive Inclusive Training Program (MRITP). Although the MRITP will provide international standard training for vulnerable populations, including migrants, at this stage, training is provided with standards recognized in former Soviet countries. BDO Academy has its own training curricula, which is accepted in Romania. The first group of 55 migrants went to Romania from November 2019 to date. It is expected that another group of 20 will leave in April 2020.

Job offers are advertised in newspapers, and interested potential migrants apply with passport, diploma, and medical report. Migrants must have no criminal record and must provide a certificate. The applicants need to take an exam to ensure that they have the necessary skills. The first group of 55 posts had 400 applications; only 70 passed the exam. Some applicants with diplomas did not pass the exams because they lacked the necessary skills, and in some sectors, the training provided was out of date.

After successfully passing the exams, migrants are assisted with visa procurement and other necessary documentation. BDO Academy charges a fee that can be paid back in installments after they receive their salaries. Salaries of unskilled migrants in a Romanian company are $510 and for skilled work $650–800, whereas professionals are paid $800–1200. Accommodation, food, and transport are free for the migrants.

Migrants receive a 5-day predeparture orientation: 2 days on law (general and workplace), 2 days on work etiquette and conditions, and 1 day on legal agreements. In addition, they also receive a 9-day orientation at the destination country on occupational safety, medical procedures, and company rules and procedures. The orientation includes family as well for some issues.

To overcome the language barriers, a team leader was created for the low-skilled migrant group, who can communicate with the management in English.

Other countries interested in employing Tajik migrants are Germany and the Republic of Korea. BDO Academy believes better training will create better job opportunities for Tajik migrants.

— Interview with Nabisher Djuraev, national MRITP coordinator, STVET, ADB, and Bakhtiyor Ahmadov, partner, BDO Academy.

products; low-interest loans (for investment); grant programs; and entrepreneurship development. Sri Lanka launches several programs for the returnee migrants such as housing scheme and industrial establishment (SLBFE). Government and financial institutions primarily sponsor these types of welfare-based programs.

Box 5:   Financial Facilities and Instruments in Bangladesh

In Bangladesh, the state-run migrant bank offers a maximum loan of $1,250 for remigration of returnees to cover the cost of airfare. It also offers up to $12,500 for reintegration with only property documents and without collateral or mortgage.

Returnees can avail loan facilities provided by other public and private banks. The Probashi Banking division of the BRAC Bank (private bank) caters to the nonresident Bangladeshi by not only facilitating remittance transfer service but also creating a favorable environment for nonresident Bangladeshis to make long-term financial contributions to the socioeconomic progress of the nation. Microfinance institutes assist migrants and their families in setting up small business and agro-based enterprises.

Source: International Organization for Migration. 2018d. *The Mapping and Scoping of Services for The Migrant Workers of Bangladesh at Various Stages of Labor Migration Cycle.* Bangladesh.

E. Psychosocial assistance for both vulnerable and returned migrants: Psychosocial well-being is important for successful reintegration back into society, it is particularly important for returnees who were deported or who are on the reentry ban list of the Russian Federation, because of the shame and failure associated with return. In the Philippines, the psychosocial component of OWWA's reintegration support includes community organizing program or organizing of OFW family circles and services such as social counseling, family counseling, stress debriefing, and training on capacity building and value formation.

F. Welfare Services: In addition to services provided to migrants at all stages of migration as well as support to family members, governments carry out other welfare programs for migrants and their families. For example, OWWA (Philippines) administers scholarship

programs for dependents of migrants, economic support to deceased migrants, repatriation of dead bodies free of cost, temporary shelter in halfway houses, and other services.

G. Legal and organizational structure: In addition to developing services, operational capacities need to be increased as well. In this context, legal and organizational structure is equally important for implementing reintegration policies and programs.

H. Assisting migrants and families within existing broad aim programs: In Tajikistan, a large number of migrants returned due to reentry ban in the Russian Federation and the labor market in Tajikistan cannot absorb such a large number of people returning to already-strained communities. In addition, women and children abandoned are also another vulnerable group. Along with direct post-return programs, some programs target vulnerable population, including migrants, in the community.

I. Matching grant program: the case of Moldova PARE 1+1 and FAO in Tajikistan.[74] The matching grant program is a popular instrument for private sector development interventions in the world. They focus on fostering small and medium enterprises' competitiveness, primarily, via the use of business development services.

The program was successfully launched and implemented in Moldova, where as recently as 2019, three out of 10 Moldovan citizens are abroad. In the program, diaspora associations, generally referred to as Home Town Associations (HTA), in partnership with the local authorities support expatriate Moldovans who are willing to contribute to the local development. These programs will offer the HTAs the possibility to obtain funding for local projects based on the 1+1 formula; the amount of the grant will be equivalent to the contribution of the Moldovan diaspora.

Based on the PARE 1+1 experience, FAO Tajikistan developed a pilot project in Hissor city and Jaloliddini Balkhi district. The project is implemented by an oversight committee involving various government

---

[74]   Interview with FAO officials, Oleg Guchgeldiyev, FAO representative in Tajikistan and Ibrohim Ahmadov, national program coordinator.

agencies, IOM, and FAO. The project is funded by the Russian Federation. The project seeks to promote inclusive economic growth through matching grants by involving migrants' remittances to invest in agriculture and agribusiness. The pilot aims to mobilize remittances and human resources of migrant workers, their families, returnees, and communities to improve their livelihood, and thus allowing beneficiaries to invest 50% of funds for small-scale business-oriented activity in agriculture or agribusiness and attract an additional 50% from the FAO project's funds. In addition to financial support, the pilot includes capacity-development programs, which allow beneficiaries to build skills in small and medium business development in the agricultural sector, such as 10-day general training and 10-day agri-business training. FAO supports beneficiaries in the preparation of investment proposals and also by advising and raising their capacity in agricultural production, storage, processing, and marketing to ensure the sustainability of the investments. To be eligible for participation in the pilot program, applicants should be migrants or returnees, women with household responsibilities receiving remittances from a first-degree relative, or forced returnees for nonthreatening administrative issues with proven ineligibility to migrate abroad.

IOM Community Stabilization and Livelihood Program: Under its community stabilization work, IOM focuses on reintegrating returned migrants with reentry bans, providing opportunities to youth, and supporting single-female-headed households of migrant families. IOM provides in-kind grants to community members in districts bordering Afghanistan in both the GBAO and Khatlon regions to start new enterprises. Many IOM-supported business ideas involve cross-border businesses, which help to stimulate trade and build relationships between Tajik and Afghan communities as well as reduce incentives for smuggling goods.[75]

In partnership with the Adult Training Centres of Tajikistan (part of the Ministry of Labor, Migration and Employment) IOM has provided vocational training to more than 800 people. Participants in the courses are primarily returned migrants, youth, and single-female heads of households. The courses, officially certified by the Ministry of Labor, Migration and Employment, have greatly improved the employment rates of vulnerable community members. The introduction of new skills into communities facing multiple challenges continues to have a stabilizing effect.

JICA's upcoming business incubation project: JICA plans to begin a project from April 2020 by developing a network of business incubators, which will enable young people, women, and returned migrants to develop small and medium businesses and thereby create jobs. State institutions will host the project and will be implemented in Dushanbe and all four regions of Tajikistan. Core activities of the project are entrepreneurship development for beneficiaries, capacity building of staff, and public awareness training on business development. JICA will coordinate with the World Bank (implementing a sister project) and the ADB MRITP program. It is hoped that the project will be sustainable and maintained by the government.[76]

Digitization of Migration Information and Services

The world is shifting to digital transformation. Technology—particularly the digital connectivity offered by mobile phones—affects every aspect of migration: it provides access to information during premigration, journeys, and in destination countries; facilitates remittances; and helps migrants stay connected to families.[77] Digital tools and platforms are used in all sectors, including the management of labor migration and services. Although some of these technologies raise concerns about privacy and security of migrants, they offer migrants easy access to information and fast and secure services. For migration management and migrant services, digitization can

---

75   IOM. *Community Stabilization and Emergencies.* http://www.iom.tj/index.php/en/activities/community-stabilization (accessed on 24 January 2020) and interview with IOM officials Michael Hewitt, project manager, and Gulnora Kamolova, project assistant.

76   Interview with Umed Kasymov, program officer, JICA Tajikistan.

77   SDC. 2018. *Technology, Migration and the 2030 Agenda for Sustainable Development.* Briefing Note. Bern.

bring efficiency, transparency, accountability, and cost-effective solutions to some migration challenges.

The combination of mobile phones, the internet, and social media—together labeled "digital connectivity"—is crucial, seen by the European Union as "a game changer for migration."[78] The low cost of smartphones and internet access, along with the proliferation of mobile networks and phone apps, has enabled even the poor (migrants and others) to use the technology (SDC 2018). The ways in which technology has facilitated migration are summarized in the Swiss Agency for Development and Cooperation (SDC) report as follows:

- information on the quality of life and economic opportunities that are available elsewhere, which shapes aspirations, decisions to migrate, and migration plans, including destination country preferences;

- essential planning and travel information on the journey itself, including transport options (official and informal such as people smugglers), transport costs, translation, and safety, including avoiding difficult borders;

- access to migrants' own or family financial resources for the journey, while in transit and upon arrival at the destination, via mobile money platforms;

- information to facilitate resettling in the destination country after arrival by accessing migrant networks and local information in the destination country;

- continuing linkages with families and networks in their country of origin through messaging, voice call, and social network apps available on mobile phones.

In addition, mobile phones help migrant to settle into a new country and society, allowing them to access a wide range of essential information and services, including housing, employment, or training opportunities; local health and transport; schools and childcare; and cultural or religious events (especially within their own diaspora community). Phones also enable migrants to engage with the authorities processing their asylum or residency claims and are a personal security mechanism for vulnerable groups

such as women domestic workers. Language learning and translation apps are increasingly used both by migrants themselves and by NGOs which provide migrant support services in many countries. Social media platforms enable migrants to connect with migrant networks in the same destination country and further afield. However, it should be noted that mobile phones are not the answer to all migrants' challenges, it provides some immediate assistance to migrants (SDC 2018).

Mobile phones also help migrants keep in touch with family and home country, allowing them political and cultural involvement. Migrants may live in the destination country, but culturally and politically they can still be part of the home country. Often termed as e-migration, some argue that strong origin-country links make integration into host country more difficult. However, it seems quite possible for migrants to simultaneously have strong ties with origin countries and be well integrated into destination countries (SDC 2018).

Mobile phones also allow continuing emotional support to (and from) family members via messaging and Voice over Internet Protocol software, as well as enabling lower cost and faster remittances to provide financial support to families. Social media is the most common software technology used by migrants and has fundamentally transformed their relationships—allowing them to both retain links with families and communities "back home" and integrate into diaspora and local communities in the destination country (SDC 2018).

In short, digitization of information is an important means of communication in all aspects of migration management and governance as well as in all stages of migration. It is an important medium in reaching more migrants, accessing remote areas, and reducing the vulnerabilities of migrants and their families.

In the area of migration management, governments in the Association of Southeast Asian Nations (ASEAN) have developed digital management systems and databases for different aspects of the

---

[78]   EPSC. 2017 Quoted in SDC. 2018.

migration process and provision of services to migrant workers. Some of the benefits include placement and processes that are smoother and faster; a reduction in time and cost; and an increase in transparency and accountability at all stages of the migration cycle.[79]

When digital management platforms also store important documents—such as work contracts, payment slips, or medical certificates—they create a record of agreements, a so-called digital trail. This feature can be useful if disputes about contract terms, repayments, or other issues arise between a migrant worker and an employer or recruitment agency.[80] In addition, online registration service for migrant workers and online and real-time databases for managing overseas employment procedures can be digitized (ADB 2020).

Box 6: Complaint and/or Feedback Management System for Migrants in the Philippines

The Overseas Workers Welfare Administration (OWWA) Electronic Case Registry and Response System (e-CARES) allows migrants to register complaints and assigns each case a reference, which allows migrants to track their complaints. e-CARES has a database of OWWA members and their contract records; OWWA members' records of predeparture educational programs, welfare assistance programs and services, and requests for assistance; an accompanying app with useful information; and an e-card for members to access benefits.

Source: International Labour Organization. 2020. Digitization and Future of Migration. Presentation at ADBI-OECD-ILO Roundtable on Labor Migration in Asia, Future of Labor Migration in Asia, Challenges and Opportunities in the Next Decade. Bangkok, 7 February.

Digital platforms can lower costs of recruitment process and increase accountability in recruitment practices. It can also help in monitoring recruitment agencies and increasing accountability. Platforms can use alerts with blacklisted recruitment agents.

Recruitment agents can use social network spaces for migrant workers to directly and publicly connect with

agents in relation to requests, issues, or complaints. Online platforms can also help migrant workers make informed choices through the use of "rate and review" platforms (ILO 2020).

Digital support can be provided to a migrant at all stages of migration: In the predeparture stage, digitization of information and services can be seen in awareness-raising programs; online recruitment and employment-oriented service platforms (e.g., LinkedIn); digital skill certification platforms; PDO via mobile apps or websites; digital booklets on language, destination country; language learning apps, websites, or YouTube videos; and many others.

At the destination country, apps and platforms can be in use to provide migrant workers with responsive, relevant, and tailored information; foster decent and productive working conditions; and address remittance costs and financial inclusion.[81]

Improving outreach, networking, and service provision—messaging apps and social media: apps such as Line, WhatsApp, Viber, and Facebook are already used to reach out to migrant workers, help them access services, and enable connecting and organizing amongst migrant workers. Using these apps is cheaper and more likely to be effective.

Mobile payment systems are addressing remittance costs and financial inclusion. Apps provide digital solutions for remittance transfer, e-banking, and mobile payments. New digital tools are increasing transparency and competition among money transfer operators, which is expected to push remittance costs down. Other digital tools include digital wallets, mobile payments, and so forth. Online tools to calculate information such as loan repayments, interest accumulation, and foreign exchange are available for migrants (ILO 2020).

At the post-arrival stage, digital programs include "helpline" apps; databases and platforms/apps to

[79] ILO. 2020. Digitization and Future of Migration. Presentation at the ADBI-OECD-ILO Roundtable on Labor Migration in Asia; Future of Labor Migration in Asia; Challenges and Opportunities in the Next Decade. Bangkok, 7 February.

[80] ILO. 2018. Op Ed. How Digitalization Can Help Achieve Fair Migration. 31 October. https://www.ilo.org/asia/media-centre/statements-and-speeches/WCMS_648541/lang--en/index.htm.

[81] ADB. 2020. Asian *Development Outlook 2020: What Drives Innovation in Asia?* Manila

manage migrant welfare (including complaints) and facilitate workers' access to justice; digital tools that promote peer-to-peer connections and collective organizing among workers; platforms that enable workers to rate and review recruiters, employers, and other intermediaries; networking and information dissemination; structures to manage migrant welfare, including reintegration services; educational technologies for upskilling and/or reskilling of return migrant workers; and digital solutions and platforms that aim to build the capacity of migrants, both for reintegration and possible re-migration (e.g., skills certification and recognition of prior learning, financial literacy, investment and small business management training programs) (ADB 2020).

Tajikistan is well positioned to take advantage of digitization to support migrant workers by the use of cell phones: 6.9 million of the total population of 9.1 million are mobile phone users. However, only 2.95 million are internet users. Compared to half (44%) of the population in Asia and the Pacific, only a third of the Tajik population are internet users.

Recommendations and Conclusion

Introduction

The main objective of this report is to identify (i) appropriate predeparture programs for Tajik migrants, including counseling on labor laws and regulations in destination countries; departure and arrival procedures; insurance and other protection services for Tajik migrants; financial literacy programs including safe banking and remittance services; and others and (ii) appropriate post-return services. Considering COVID-19's adverse effects on the economy, the report also proposes some pandemic-related recommendations. In addition to the recommendations on predeparture and post-return services, described in the following sections, it is recommended that study tours to one of the labor-origin countries in Asia (discussed in the report) could be organized for relevant MOLME departments/agencies to gather experience on migration management good practices.

Some specific recommendations and remedies are not covered in this report. These are the plight of the women and children left behind; exclusion from the pension system; high cost of passports and migration; difficulties and cost of acquiring a work permit and work patent in the Russian Federation; lack of savings and investment by the migrants (including lack of trust in the banking system); low-skilled migration resulting in low wages; work environment in destination countries; need for enhanced legal support to migrants in need; free online courses; awareness of training and its relevance in gainful employment to increase skilled migration, which will reduce low-skilled migration, which in turn will reduce risks.

Remedies to these problems require bilateral dialogue, already being undertaken by the governments.

However, some issues require developing a process, for example, inclusion of migrants in the pension system, to allow them a dignified life after retirement. Further research into these areas is highly recommended to reduce the vulnerabilities of migrant workers and their families.

Another challenge is the shortage of MOLME representatives in the destination countries; if there are no supporting services for migrants, they will not be motivated to participate in the orientation. PDOS will not be as effective if it only provides information to the migrants about working conditions, culture, and law without developing supporting programs. For example, if the migrants are not paid, they need the option of accessing legal aid, either provided by the MOLME or the embassies, or through NGOs or migrant/diaspora associations that support migrant workers in destination countries.

Although outside the direct scope of this report, it is recommended that the number of MOLME representatives be increased, provided with diplomatic status and training on what services are available and how to provide services to migrants. Existing migrant networks are also excellent resources in the destination countries and MOLME or the embassy should tap into these resources. Migrant networks possess transnational knowledge of both origin and destination country and have emotional ties with new migrants, as well as insight into the diverse local realities in which they participate. They can be an organized resource both in developing digital resources for migrants and in post-arrival orientation at the destination countries.

Recommendations on Predeparture Services

Predeparture services should be catered to potential and returned migrants, their families, as well as communities. Tajik migration is often a family decision, wherein community and clan leaders have significant influence. A primary service in predeparture stage is the PDOS.

For Tajikistan, a primary challenge for the PDO lies in motivating migrants to take the course. As discussed in Chapter 3, because registration and PDOS are mandatory in the selected Asian countries (Bangladesh, Indonesia, Nepal, the Philippines, and Sri Lanka), managing registration and PDO participation is easier. In addition, as the major destination countries require visa for entrance, migrants can be denied exit permit at border points in their home countries without proof of registration and PDOS participation. For Tajikistan, the major destination countries are within the region, where a visa is not required for entrance. In this instance, awareness-raising programs, PEOS, and digital information can alert migrants to the necessity of undertaking a PDOS. Also, incentives such as those discussed in Chapter 3 (access of registrant to free insurance coverage and payment of embarkation tax and welfare benefits, such as access to loans from state banks at subsidized interest rates and scholarships for children) could also be included.

As suggested by the ADB (2019a) report, the PDOS should be carried out with a clear view of understanding the effect of PDOS. The overall quantifiable and unquantifiable benefits of the program for migrants (and their families) who received the services (treatment group) should be compared with those who have not received these services (control group). In this case, the project should offer PDOS as a package with the expectation that beneficiaries participate in all modules. As discussed, PDOS provides information that will be needed in all three stages of migration (predeparture, post-arrival, and return and reintegration), as well as the well-being

of the family left behind.[82] The other predeparture services recommended in the report are awareness-raising programs; skill recognition and skills training; training on general and occupational safety; English and destination country-specific language training; PEOS; and job finding in the local and overseas markets.

These recommendations are discussed in brief as follows: Awareness-raising programs on safe migration can be conducted by the government, international organizations, and nongovernment actors. Awareness-raising programs should use media such as mobile apps, websites, TV, radio, newspaper, popular theater shows, job fairs, rallies, and community-level meetings. Printed materials, such as posters, brochures, booklets, and leaflets, could be developed for dissemination. Audio and audio-visual materials such as advertisements and drama could be disseminated through TV. "Religious leaders and key figures in the communities could be sensitized in raising awareness of potential and return migrants." [83]

The main objective of the awareness-raising campaign should be to provide information on the costs and benefits of migration, available options for developing one's skills and realities of migration. It should also encourage migrants to register and participate in the PDO and inform about digital apps, advantages of skills training, and options in job markets.

Skill training and skill recognition: Jobs in demand in the destination countries should be identified and training should be upgraded and/or developed accordingly. It is also important to improve the quality and relevance of training and to develop training that meets the needs of employers in the countries of destination and/or international standard. Collaboration of training providers and recruiting agencies and employers abroad will ensure that graduates meet the requirements for employment.

In addition, many migrants already have skill sets recognized by competent authorities. A recognized

---

[82]   Appendix 3 discusses in detail the basic propositions, training topics, methodology of development and updating of PDOS, PDOS structure, selection criteria of trainers, recommendations on TOT, monitoring and evaluation of the training, and management of the PDOS.

[83]   Interview with Nabisher Djuraev, national MRITP coordinator, ADB-funded Strengthening Technical and Vocational Education and Training Project.

diploma will assist the migrants in securing well-paid employment abroad. For skills acquired outside of the education system, a system of recognition of skills in their home country will allow migrants to have such skills certified. Mutual recognition agreements between the country of origin and countries of destination are also necessary to ensure that such certifications are recognized abroad. Training should be aligned to the skills standards of countries of destination to ensure mutual recognition of degrees.

According to the research, even when authorities are available to recognize skills and develop skills at low or free of cost, the information is not always available to potential or return migrants. Both of these options should be a component of awareness-raising programs. Most migrants are low skilled, which results in low wage, which in turn results in dependency on remigration. To break this circle, migrants should be made aware of available skill development and enhancement opportunities of international standard. Stakeholders recommend that procedures of acquired skill (gained in the destination countries) recognition be established by the government. This will include a system of assessment and certification of acquired skills. Vocational training institutes can be enabled to take over this role.

Registration of migrant workers is another area that needs focus, as there is no mandatory registration for migrants (therefore, detail data on migration are difficult to achieve), which would have aided the government in identifying areas of focus and inform policy interventions. Digital technology can be used to assist migrants in registering and reducing time and could also be done at a distance from the center.

Training on general and occupational safety should be included in all skills training or be a part of PDOS. The following three areas should be included: i) general health and safety procedures, ii) occupational health and safety procedures, and iii) first aid. The general and occupational safety training could be provided by external trainers (Red Cross/Crescent, employers, and others) based on standard criteria.

Language training: Migrant workers identified language training as the most important need for Tajik migrants. Both skilled and unskilled workers highlighted the need to learn the destination-country language. Although the need for destination-country-specific language is important, the need for English was also highlighted. The language needs of migrants have the following four broad categories: (i) a life skill; (ii) legal requirements; (iii) work; and (iv) personal safety, well-being, and justice.

Destination-country-specific general language training should be combined with skill-specific language training. For example, training for nurses in Bangladesh included topics on interacting with patients and visitors; establishing relationships with patients and colleagues; communicating with doctors, supervisors, and management; workplace harassment; and standard of care.[84]

Although Tajiks are required to gain a language certificate in Russian language either in the Russian Federation or in Tajikistan, many unskilled migrants do not require this certificate. It is proposed that a migrant-specific language program be developed to assist them in dealing with day-to-day life in the destination country. Since Tajiks have a basic understanding of the Russian language, self-learning by electronic means can be developed. In addition to any destination-country language, a digital app for learning basic English words should be developed.

Printed and downloadable phrase books should be developed in major destination-country-specific language as well as English, which will provide critical words and phrases for survival.

Preemployment orientation seminar is a more targeted orientation program than awareness raising. PEOS programs can be carried out in schools, all technical and vocational education training institutes, including, ALCs and initial VET (IVET) institutes, job centers, local government-level institutions, and so on. PEOS is a bridge between awareness-raising programs and PDOS.

---

[84] IOM. 2006. *English Language Manual for Skilled Migrant Workers.* Dhaka.

The government and private sectors can play a significant role in job finding for migrants in the local and overseas labor markets. Whereas placement in the local market will assist return migrants in integrating into the society, overseas job placement can ensure better protection for both returned (who wants to re-migrate) and potential migrants.

Recommendations on Post-Return Services

During the course of the research, the Migration Service was providing most of its assistance to the migrants in the reentry ban list of the Russian Federation. This report recommends some services to be developed as post-return services for migrants in the Russian Federation's reentry ban list and for return migrants who are planning to settle down or re-migrate.

The recommendations are divided into two parts: first, short-term recommendations specific to deported migrants and migrants in the reentry ban list of the Russian Federation and second, medium- and long-term recommendations for all return migrants.

Short-Term Recommendations Specific to Deported Migrants and Migrants on the Reentry Ban List of the Russian Federation

Immediate assistance needs to be provided to migrant workers who have been expelled or denied entry by Russian authorities at the border. IOM research (2014a) has shown that expelled migrants and migrants who were turned down at Russian airports form the most vulnerable category and suffer especially during their first weeks after return, notably from psychological stress. The same research also identifies that the existing support opportunities are insufficient because they do not address these returned migrants' immediate needs. The staff of the air companies, Tajik Border Guards, and other relevant staff at the airports of Dushanbe, Khujand, Qurghonteppa, and Kulob need to be trained on how to provide these migrant workers with immediate assistance in terms of information and consultation,

referral, reintegration support opportunities and, if needed, psychosocial help (IOM 2014a).

Linking existing return and reintegration programs by the development partners, private sector, and NGOs to migrants. In the short term, legal assistance, psychosocial support, promotion of employment, recognition of skills of migrants, inclusion in skill development programs, entrepreneurship development programs, and other existing programs carried out by different stakeholders should be actively pursued by the Migration Service to assist the migrants in reintegrating in the country.

Medium- and Long-Term Recommendations for Return Migrants

For migrants in the reentry ban list of the Russian Federation

Improved cooperation between migration authorities of Tajikistan and the Russian Federation could reduce the difficulties for migrants in the reentry ban list. Since many migrants find out their name has been added only after they reach their destination, this will ensure that migrants are properly informed about their legal status before departure. Since the individual inquiry of migrant workers about reentry bans at the Russian Federal Migration Service and Federal Security Service is very time-consuming and complicated, the Government of Tajikistan can enter negotiations with the Government of the Russian Federation to share its list of Tajik citizens with reentry bans with relevant Tajik counterparts, such as the Migration Service and the border guards, on a more regular (at least monthly) basis. Providing a recent list every month would simplify responding to inquiries of migrant workers and ultimately help them readjust their future plans as early as possible (IOM 2014a).

Implement early-warning mechanisms for Tajik migrant workers with reentry bans. Only a fraction of all migrant workers with reentry bans investigate their status on their own initiative. Most migrants continue to leave Tajikistan as they are not aware of their status. They only become aware of the situation when they are denied entry at Russian airports and border checkpoints. A system that automatically informs migrants about their reentry bans will reduce the cost of time and money, as well as psychological shock at the destination country border points. Examples include a software program for use by the Tajik border forces that informs Tajik citizens returning from or leaving for the Russian Federation about their reentry bans, if any, or another for use by airline companies that notifies them if a prospective passenger booking a flight to the Federation is on the list (IOM 2014a).

Develop a return policy for migrants from deportation centers and other vulnerable migrants to address their medical, legal, psychosocial needs. The return policy should address all needs of a migrant at the stages of predeparture to Tajikistan, during travel and post-return at home.

For return migrants

Set up legal aid services, referral to legal aid agencies, as well as free legal assistance for Tajik migrants.

Explore new labor markets and create overseas employment opportunities for destination countries other than those in CIS. A primary reason Tajiks travel to CIS countries, particularly the Russian Federation, is social capital. Government and private sector efforts to create new labor markets will assist the migrants in finding new job opportunities. It should be noted that this recommendation may be more motivating for the migrants in the reentry ban list of the Russian Federation; if they do not have family in the Russian Federation or any other motivation to go back, they would be motivated to seek overseas employment in a different country.

Create skill development and skill recognition programs targeting returned migrants to reduce the majority of migrant workers from Tajikistan being employed in low-skilled jobs. This has been discussed in more detail in Recommendations on Predeparture Services.

Develop small and medium business assistance programs. One motivator for returning migrants is the desire to run their own business; however, migrants are often not aware of the legal, economic (low-interest loans, taxes, etc.) and administrative requirements needed to begin a new venture. Awareness-raising

and training programs on running small and medium businesses should be linked with existing programs and developed if needed.

Develop low-interest loan packages and grant programs for skill development, remigration, and economic activities.

Assist in psychosocial reintegration and readjustment to family and community. Psychosocial assistance is needed for both vulnerable migrants and returned migrants in normal circumstances; however, the program will have to take into account their different needs.

Increase awareness about existing reintegration opportunities of Migration Service and other organizations. Updated electronic information will assist migrants identify what is available as reintegration assistance.

Develop legal and institutional structures—in addition to programs—for management of return and reintegration programs.

Recommendations on Digitizing Migration Information and Services

Given that Tajikistan is a mountainous country with majority of the migrants originating from rural areas, developing mobile apps for and providing the same information through the Migration Service website will prove cost-effective for migrants. Online programs and networks will also bring important data in the district and *jamoat* levels to the fingertips of policy-makers.

Establishing district- or *jamoat*-level centers in remote areas will not be possible right away and may not be cost-effective. Therefore, digital apps should be developed to assist migrant workers in registering with the government, search for jobs, and acquire information to assist them in making informed decisions about migration, predeparture information and formalities, support services at the destination countries, and post-return services. Because of difficulties in reaching seasonal migrants, they should be targeted through digital technology as well as through mass media awareness raising. However, digital information cannot replace face-to-face training and should be complementary to the government's regular program. The following are possible digital services:

- At the predeparture stage, all relevant information on safe migration dissemination (including cost-benefits of migration, realities in destination countries, and destination-country-specific information, such as salary, law, culture, weather, work environment, and family needs while abroad should be provided. All PDOS information and Immigration and Customs Enforcement (ICE) materials and language and destination-country-specific booklets should be uploaded as a referral.

- At the destination country, in addition to destination-country-specific information, provide requirements of consular and other services (for example, legal) and name and contact details of all MOLME representatives.

- At the post-return stage, cross-check with the reentry ban list of the Russian Federation before departure and provide information on redress mechanisms, legal provisions, documentation requirements, and so forth. Information on remittance investment, entrepreneurship development training, grant programs, loan programs, and so forth can also be included.

Services across different stages of migration, as well as for families left behind and abandoned spouses and children, could include the following:

- Online registration of migrants. Traveling to the center from a remote area to register is not cost-effective and therefore not an incentive for migrants. Online platforms, with support from an awareness-raising program, should encourage more migrants to register. The registration database should be updated with job, contract, diploma, and other relevant information.

- Creation of a database of return migrants.

- Provision of information on available migrant services in destination countries and in Tajikistan.

- Provision of information on legal assistance or referral service availability.

- Development of destination-country-specific and migrant-focused language apps. Existing apps such as "Busuu" and "Duolingo" could become a baseline to design such programs.

- Provision of regular updates of skill recognition, skill enhancement, and new skill development information from ALCs and other training institutes.

- Linking recruiting agencies with potential and returned migrants for overseas employment.

- Offer of job matching with migration/recruitment agencies or at local market, using the database of registration.

In addition, general and specific queries, frequently asked questions, and other features should be uploaded in the digital apps and platforms. Information should regularly be updated on both the apps and the websites. All government agencies also must provide a standardized content, for example, MOLME's information regarding consular services cannot be different from the information provided by other ministries.

Recommendations on Managing Labor Migration during and after the COVID-19 Pandemic

The Government of Tajikistan can devise short-, medium- and long-term strategies to reduce the unforeseen effects of the pandemic. For all strategies and consequent programs, the government must consider migrants, their families, and the vulnerable population within migration, such as unaccompanied or separated children, women and girls, elderly, persons with disabilities or other medical vulnerabilities, survivors of gender-based violence, and other vulnerable groups in need of protection.

Short Term

- Provide assistance to migrant workers who are in the destination countries and unable to return. Assistance could be ensuring access of affected people to basic needs, such as food, shelter, healthcare (including psychosocial), and safety and protection.

- Negotiate with destination country governments to release migrants from detention centers for irregularity and repatriate them.

- Assist stranded migrants to return home.

- Provide immediate grants to families left behind who are in need, as well as vulnerable migrants in the destination countries.

- Provide awareness-raising programs on migrant health with particular focus on being safe during the COVID-19 outbreak.

Medium Term

- Formulate strategies—in coordination with destination-country governments and employers, to continue labor migration after travel bans are relaxed, ensuring safety of all countries involved. An option might be to reskill and upskill migrants to move from low-demand sectors to high-demand sectors during the pandemic (for example, essential services in food supply, agriculture, transport, healthcare, etc.).

- Negotiate with destination countries to include migrant workers in their health system, particularly for those who cannot come back and those who will need to newly or re-migrate.

- Include migrant workers in the social protection schemes of the home country.

- Undertake steps to assist migrants in sending remittances electronically and in inexpensive ways to avoid informal money transfers.

- Assist returned migrant workers to find employment or other income-generating activities within the country. Relevant short-term training on high-demand jobs can ensure timely employment of returned migrants.

- Assist future migrants to newly migrate or return to destination countries.

- Seek strategies to reduce the risks of contagion until vaccines are widely administered. For example, overcrowded train travel during seasonal migration to the Russian Federation should be one of the issues taken into consideration for continuing migration to the country.

Expand mobile network coverage; making internet access inexpensive will assist the government in providing migration-related and general information to its population.

Long Term

- Prepare to take advantage of the economic recovery by analyzing future labor trends and training the population accordingly. For example, an immediate need will be for healthcare professionals, not only doctors.

- Prepare a strategy to address future situations similar to the current pandemic.

Conclusion: Migration is an important livelihood option for Tajik migrants. As an alternative to local employment, migration has been practiced for decades. Migrant remittances are an economic lifeline to poor households in many countries; a decrease in remittance flows could increase poverty and reduce households' access to much-needed health services (KNOMAD 2020). Although this report focuses on challenges, the positive outcomes of migration should not be ignored. Addressing the challenges will bring further positive outcomes for migrants, their families, the community, and ultimately the country. In the coming years, Tajikistan will need to undertake many of the recommendations; however—considering the global pandemic and its adverse effects on labor migration—some steps need to be taken immediately. Digitization of information, particularly in this time of social distancing, can play a vital role in creating awareness among populations as well as informing migrants of job and training opportunities, general awareness, and many other issues.

List of Persons Interviewed for the Report

Government of Tajikistan (in order of date/time interviewed)
1. Saidov Saidasror Haqnazarovich, Head of Department of Migration and Population, MOLME
2. Safarzoda Khushbakht, Head of the Legal Department, MOLME
3. Amirbekzooda Mehrobsho, Deputy Director, Labor and Employment Agency, MOLME
4. Karimzoda Tohir, Director, Migration Service
5. Sharipov Tolib, Deputy Director, Migration Service
6. Abdullaev Sharif, Head of Department of International Relations, Migration Service
7. Saidov Saidbeg, Director of Pre-Departure Center for Migrants, Migration Services

Development Partners, Private Sector, and CSOs (in order of date/time interviewed)
8. Abduaziz Kasymov, Deputy Director, Z Analytics Group
9. Baqozoda Kahramo, Director, Z Analytics Group
10. Beknazarova Gulnora, Analytic Expert, Z Analytics Group
11. Umed Kasymov, Program Officer, JICA
12. Oleg Guchgeldiyev; FAO Representative in Tajikistan
13. Ibrohim Ahmadov, National Program Coordinator, FAO
14. Michael Hewitt, Project Manager, IOM Tajikistan
15. Gulnora Kamolova, Project Assistant, IOM Tajikistan
16. Bakhtiyor Ahmadov, Partner, BDO Academy

Project administration group (PAG)–MOLME, ADB Project
17. Abdulmajid Bobokhonov, Consultant Team Leader, ADB STVET Project
18. Ismatulloev Ismatullo Ubaydovich, Deputy Team Leader, TRTA, SEEP
19. Kuddusov Jamshed, Labor Economist, TRTA, SEEP
20. Shafarov Shokir, National Coordinator, PAG
21. Nabisher Djuraev, National MRITP Coordinator, STVET

Other
22. Nurul Islam, Director (retired), BMET

Migrants

FGDs with 32 migrants were held in Migration Services offices twice, 4 and 7 February 2020. All migrants were male and were on the list of reentry ban to the Russian Federation. Their origin districts/cities are Rudaki district, Vahdat city, Tusunzoda city, Firdavsi district, Dushanbe, Sino district, Jomi district, and Fayzobod.

In addition, Nahreen Farjana participated in two meetings on 4 and 5 February 2020. These meetings provided valuable information on the different government ministry and department roles as well as future policies in Tajikistan. The meeting held on 4 February was attended by MOLME representatives including the Honorable Minister, government ministries, and departments and ADB PAG office relevant department representatives to discuss the ADB STVET project and the new ADB SEEP project. The meeting on 5 February was a roundtable; participating were representatives of relevant government ministries and departments and international organizations. These meetings provided valuable information on the different government ministry and department roles as well as future policies in Tajikistan.

Legal Instruments and Relevant Stakeholders in Migration Management in Tajikistan

Legal Instruments in Migration Management

Migration in Overall Development Planning

The National Development Strategy of the Republic of Tajikistan for the period up to 2030 (NDS 2030) sets a target of increasing domestic incomes by up to 3.5 times by 2030 and reducing poverty by half (NDS 2030). As two main activities for reaching its goals, the government has identified diversification of foreign labor migration, including from a gender perspective, and strengthened state regulation of migrants' return process (NDS 2030, p. 11).

In 2016, the government identified the high social cost of labor migration and a decrease in the volume of remittances sent by migrant workers as challenges for development (NDS 2030). The strategy highlights two factors causing high social cost: social protection of migrant workers in the destination country and deepening social problems in migrants' families that remain in the home country (NDS 2030, p. 29).

In ensuring equal opportunities and the reduction of social inequality in Tajikistan, foreign labor migration of men has been identified as a major problem with direct gender implications, including the problem of abandoned women and children, particularly in rural areas (NDS 2030, p. 63). Gender equality, via ensuring equal opportunities and reducing social inequalities, has also been stressed.

NDS 2030 seeks to develop services including professional development (p. 36), training of migrants (p. 75), pensions for migrant workers (p. 56), and special programs targeted at low-skilled returning migrants. Diversification of foreign labor migration and improving the impact of vocational education is also pointed to as a priority in the area of productive employment policy (p. 76).

In the area of diversification of foreign labor migration, NDS 2030 identified the following:

- development of a gender-sensitive system of predeparture training for migrant workers and their families, including legal and information support and short-term vocational and language training based on resource centers;
- development of labor migration legal and social protection programs.

The following results are expected:

- increased awareness and professional skills to work at the foreign labor markets;
- increased social welfare of migrant workers and their family members.

In addition to ensuring better migration services and opportunities, NDS 2030 reiterated the negative impact of migration: There remains a lack of qualified professionals, skilled workers, and specialists because of educational problems and the continuing migration of qualified personnel. Actively decreasing the number of migrant workers by creating employment, developing infrastructure, and creating better conditions is also part of the overall NDS 2030.

Strategies on Migration

For the first time, the National Strategy of Labor Migration of Nationals of the Republic of Tajikistan Abroad for 2011–2015 acknowledged that external labor migration presents not only challenges but also positives.[1] It contributes to establishing Tajikistan as a market of air and auto transportation, developing an active banking sector, developing trade, improving the culture of travel, and increasing the level of professional qualifications of migrant workers. The strategy also notes that the "priority of the economic policy of the country is development of the sphere of employment in Tajikistan, opening of new productive jobs while labor migration abroad is a temporary opportunity to reduce stress in internal labor market."

The State Strategy of Labor Market of the Republic of Tajikistan until 2020 provides an analysis of the situation of labor migration; it acknowledges that labor migration helps to reduce stress in the local labor market. The strategy notes that not only is labor migration increasing, but reducing it in the near future will not be possible. Nonetheless, none of the four priority objectives of the strategy have specific provisions about the improvement of services provided to migrant workers and potential migrant workers such as social insurance, organized recruitment for jobs abroad, guaranteed labor contract before departure from the country, and other measures through which the state can reduce the current risks of labor migration.

An updated version of the National Migration Strategy has been drafted but not approved by the relevant political structures as of date.

Law on Migration

Labor migration is influenced and directly or indirectly regulated by the following laws[2]:

- Law on Migration (1999)
- Law on Licensing Certain Types of Activities (2007)
- Labor Code
- Law on Promoting Employment of Population (2003)
- Law on Education (2013)

- Law on Training of Specialists Taking into the Needs of the Labor Market (2012)
- Law on Primary Vocational Education
- Law on Adult Education (2017)

The Law of the Republic of Tajikistan On Migration (1999) mainly regulates the issues of entry of foreign citizens and stateless persons permanently residing outside Tajikistan into its territory for paid work under an employment contract (agreement). It also regulates issues of obtaining work permits in Tajikistan, tracking immigration quotas, and attracting foreign labor. The law states the procedure for recognizing individuals as repatriates, internally displaced persons, and re-emigrants. Partially, the law also regulates the direction of the workforce abroad. It states that citizens of the Republic of Tajikistan who go abroad to get paid work must have an employment contract (agreement) concluded with the employer.

However, the requirement that a prospective labor migrant must have an employment contract is not enforced by the authorities. The law does not have provisions regarding the regulation of the departure of labor force abroad, the creation of mechanisms for the social protection of migrants, the creation of conditions for them to obtain the necessary qualifications, and the creation of a system of organized training for such a labor force.

The Law of the Republic of Tajikistan on Licensing Certain Types of Activities and the regulation on the specifics of licensing certain types of activities, approved by the Decree of the Government of the Republic of Tajikistan on 3 April 2007, No. 172, regulate the implementation of activities related to the job placement of citizens of the Republic of Tajikistan outside their homeland and activities pertaining to the employment of foreign citizens within the territory of the Republic of Tajikistan.

---

[1]   The key points of the National Strategy of Labor Migration of Nationals of the Republic of Tajikistan Abroad for 2011–2015 has been gathered from ADB. 2019a. *Skills and Employability Enhancement Project (SEEP), Republic of Tajikistan; TA Draft Final Report.*

[2]   The analysis of the laws is collected from ADB. 2019a. *Skills and Employability Enhancement Project (SEEP), Republic of Tajikistan; TA Draft Final Report.*

Table A2:   Tajikistan's Ratifications of International Migration Laws

International Law	Ratification	Status
Migration for Employment Convention (Revised), 1949 - ILO Convention 97	10 April 2007	In force
Migrant Workers (Supplementary Provisions) Convention (ILO Convention 143), 1975	10 April 2007	In force
International Convention on the Protection of the Rights of All Migrant Workers and Members of their Families (ICRMW or 1990 UN Migrant Rights Convention)	8 January 2002	Entry into force on 1 July 2003, in accordance with article 87

Source: International Labour Organization.

International Instruments

Tajikistan has ratified all relevant conventions[3] related to the protection of migrants, which shows the commitment of the government in upholding the rights of migrant workers (see Table A2).

Bilateral Treaties

Treaty between Tajikistan and the Russian Federation: The Government of Tajikistan has entered a treaty with the Government of the Russian Federation regarding the regulation of migration and the rights of migrants from both countries. The treaty governs labor issues and the protection of the rights of migrant workers from among citizens of the Russian Federation and the Republic of Tajikistan (2004) temporarily working in the territory of the other party's state (ADB 2019a). Key points[4] of the treaty of interest are as follows:

- The parties' competent authorities shall form a working group to resolve issues related to the implementation of this Treaty.
- Entry, exit, and stay of workers in the territory of the host state shall be regulated by the laws of the host state and this Treaty.
- Workers shall carry out temporary labor activity in the host state on the basis of a corresponding document issued in accordance with the legislation of the host state for no more than 1 year ("work permit"). The term of the work permit may be extended, but for no more than 1 year.
- Remuneration of workers shall not be lower, and working conditions less favorable, than those established for citizens of the host state who have the same position, area of concentration and qualification, and perform similar work.
- Each of the Parties shall recognize (without legalization) diplomas, certificates of education, relevant documents confirming a rank, a category, a qualification, and other documents necessary for the implementation of temporary labor activity, certified in the manner established in the territory of the state of permanent residence.
- When a worker leaves the host state, the employer or the customer of works (services) shall issue a corresponding document, certified by the seal, containing information on the duration of work and wages on a monthly basis.
- The worker has the right to social protection in accordance with the laws of the host state.
- In the event that a formal decision is made to revoke a work permit, including due to the worker performing other paid work in addition to that specified in the work permit, he/she must leave the territory of the host state within 15 days in accordance with the laws of the host state and the provisions of this Treaty (ADB 2019a).

In addition, in December 2019, the Russian Federation ratified an agreement on the organized recruitment

---

[3]   The Government of Tajikistan has not ratified the Convention concerning Decent Work for Domestic Workers, 2011 (ILO Convention 189). However, there is not much record of migration of domestic workers.

[4]   The key points of the treaty are gathered from ADB. 2019a. *Skills and Employability Enhancement Project (SEEP), Republic of Tajikistan; TA Draft Final Report.*

of Tajik labor migrants who work seasonally in the country. The agreement was signed in April 2019, but was not ratified by the Russian Federation until December of the same year. However, the process of implementation is yet to begin.

Relevant Stakeholders in Tajikistan

Relevant Major Government Institutions

The Ministry of Labor, Migration and Employment (MOLME) is charged principally with labor, migration, and technical and vocational education of labor. The Department of Migration and the Migration Services under the MOLME are directly responsible for dealing with migration issues. In addition, the Agency for Labor and Employment under MOLME and technical and vocational education and training institutes under different government agencies are also related to migration issues. Other relevant government institutions (but not limited to) directly or indirectly involved in migration management in Tajikistan are the Ministry of Health and Social Pension and the Agency for Social Insurance and Pension, the Interior Ministry; the Ministry of Foreign Affairs, the Ministry of Education and Science, and the National Bank of Tajikistan.

A. Ministry of Labor, Migration and Employment (MOLME), formerly Ministry of Labor and Social Protection: MOLME is the central executive body of state authority, responsible for the development and implementation of a uniform state policy and normative legal regulation in the field of labor migration, labor market, employment, standard of living, initial vocational education, and adult education.

The Migration Department of MOLME is responsible for developing policies and strategies on migration, whereas Migration Services is in charge of implementing the policies and strategies concerning migration issues. There is also a State agency, the Agency for the Provision of Work Abroad, under

the MOLME whose activities are aimed at providing employment for Tajik citizens, including youth, abroad.

The Pre-Departure Center for Migrants[5] under the Migration Services in Dushanbe was established by Government Decree No. 390 dated 4 June, 2014 and included in the list of organizations of the MOLME Migration Service, its founding institution. As an advisory body, the Center provides services to labor migrants to help them to prepare for migration and adapt to new conditions.

The aforementioned Decree no. 390 also mandated Migration Services to establish up to 10 predeparture service centers for migrants in different parts of Tajikistan. To date, four of these centers have been established—Dushanbe Pre-Departure Service Center and three other similar centers in Bokhtar (Khatlon Region), Khorog (GBAO), and Khujand (Sughd Region).

Box A2:   Labor Migrants, Assistance in Dushanbe, Tajikistan

The purpose of the Dushanbe center is to provide practical assistance to labor migrants through training courses and counseling and organizational and financial assistance at two stages of labor migration:

Before departure:

   (i)   organizing registration;

   (ii)   teaching destination country language, history, customs, culture, and legislation basics;

   (iii) informing about occupations in demand,

   (iv) coordinating with domestic and foreign technical and vocational lyceums (including those in the Russian Federation);

   (v)   undertaking research of the destination country labor market;

   (vi) organizing recruitment of labor migrants; and (vii) assisting in job placement abroad for Tajik citizens.

After return:

   (i)   registering returned migrants;

   (ii)   organizing medical examination;

---

5   ADB. 2019a. Skills and Employability Enhancement Project (SEEP), *Republic of Tajikistan; TA Draft Final Report;* and Quddusov. 2011. *Evaluation of Services Provided to Labor Migrants by Dushanbe Pre-Departure Service Center.*

(iii) arranging the formalization of professional skills acquired during migration;

(iv) coordinating and cooperating with technical and vocational educational institutions on retraining;

(v) informing returned labor markets on job offers;

(vi) providing assistance in business activities;

(vii) obtaining bank loans to start a business;

(viii) rendering financial assistance for returned migrants' socioeconomic adaptation.

Financed through special funds of the Migration Service, the Center also has the right to carry out entrepreneurial activities and raise funds from other sources.

Source: Quddusov. 2011. *Evaluation of Services Provided to Labor Migrants by Dushanbe Pre-Departure Service Center.* Unpublished.

The Agency of Labor and Employment is a special structure of MOLME, whose main mission is to provide employment to Tajiks. Its main functions include promoting employment, mediation in the labor migration, developing skills of unemployed people, conducting job fairs, and advertising overseas job vacancies through the Migration Service.

Technical and Vocational Education Training Institutes:[6] The Initial VET (IVET) system is under MOLME, with the Ministry of Education and Science (MOES) responsible for the secondary technical and vocational education and training (TVET) system and licensing of Initial TVET institutions and approval of Initial TVET programs.

In addition to the IVET institutions, MOLME operates 35 Adult Learning Centers (ALCs), which offer short courses of up to 6 months duration for basic skills training and skills upgrading. There are 49 secondary TVET institutions (technical colleges), which are managed by different ministries and state-owned enterprises including the MOES (20); Ministry of Culture (6); Ministry of Agriculture (2); Ministry of Health and Social Protection (15); Ministry of Energy and Water Resources (3); Ministry of Industry & New Technologies (1); Tajik Aluminium Plant (1);

Hydropower Station of Rogun (1); and the Tourism Development Committee under the government (1). The technical colleges offer 3- and 4-year courses designed to develop technicians, foremen and women, and supervisors. Additionally, the senior secondary TVET colleges tend to be significantly better equipped than the IVET lyceums, which is one of the reasons secondary TVET is more prestigious than IVET.

B. Ministry of Education and Science: The Ministry of Education and Science (MOES) is the principal ministry responsible for matters related to education in Tajikistan, including early childhood and higher education. MEOS is also responsible for some TVET programs as mentioned previously.

C. Ministry of Foreign Affairs and consular services in the destination countries: Functions to protect the rights of citizens of Tajikistan abroad are first of all vested onto the diplomatic representations of the country. According to the provisions of the Consular Charter, the consuls should "take measures to ensure that natural and legal persons of the Republic of Tajikistan fully enjoyed all the rights granted to them by the legislation of the host State, applicable international norms and practices ...".[7] Other responsibilities include representing the interests of citizens of the Republic of Tajikistan in the state bodies of the host countries (Article 28), consulting the Republic of Tajikistan citizens abroad (Article 26), assisting citizens with documents and papers (Article 36). From the perspective of human rights, the priority function of consuls is to help and assist the citizens of the Republic of Tajikistan kept under arrest or in custodial institutions abroad (Article 35) (HRC 2014).

In the Russian Federation, Tajikistan has one embassy (Moscow) and three consulates (in Moscow, Yekaterinburg, and Ufa). There are also honorary consuls in the cities of Kaliningrad, Petrozavodsk, and St. Petersburg.[8] Compared to the number of migrant workers employed in the Russian Federation,

---

[6] Information regarding the TVET institutes are gathered from ADB. 2019a. *Skills and Employability Enhancement Project (SEEP), Republic of Tajikistan; TA Draft Final Report.*

[7] Art. 23 of Consular Statute of the Republic of Tajikistan. Quoted in HRC. 2014. *Legal Protection of Migrant Workers from Tajikistan in the Russian Federation.* Dushanbe.

[8] HRC. 2014. *Legal Protection of Migrant Workers from Tajikistan in the Russian Federation.* Dushanbe.

the number of consular officers and MOLME representatives is very low.[9]

D. National Bank of Tajikistan: The Central Bank is engaged in developing policies to promote financial inclusion.

E. Ministry of Health and Social Pension and Agency for Social Insurance and Pension under the government: Responsible for social insurance and pension for Tajik citizens.

F. Interior Ministry: Responsible for granting passports to Tajik citizens.

Development Partners

A number of development partners administer programs targeted toward migrants and their families. Some such organizations with existing programs for migrants and/or their families are Asian Development Bank, DVV International, European Union, Food and Agriculture Organization, International Organization for Migration, Japan International Cooperation Agency, United Nations Development Programme (UNDP) Community Program, Tajikistan, and UN Women.

Civil Society Actors

A. CSOs and NGOs in the Russian Federation: Some NGOs provide legal, conciliation, and advisory support to migrant workers. One such NGO providing support is "Migratsiya i zakon" (Migration and Law).

B. NGOs in Tajikistan: A number of NGOs provide a range of services from the predeparture stage (e.g., awareness raising) to the post-arrival stage (e.g., providing business loan and training to run businesses).

C. Formal and informal migrant associations: In addition to Tajik construction brigades, farmer associations, and the influence of clan, discussed in Role of Migrant Networks, diaspora networks are also prevalent in the post-Soviet-era destination countries.

According to the Migration Department (MOLME), there are about 63 registered diaspora associations in the Russian Federation and two in Kazakhstan. Diaspora networks also publish information cards and leaflets for migrants on legal questions and provide some consoling and legal assistance (HRC 2014). The Embassy in Moscow liaises with 70 diasporas in different regions, some leaders of the diaspora are also on the supervisory board at the embassy (HRC 2014). In St. Petersburg, under the Migration Service, there is a supervisory board, involving all major diasporas of St. Petersburg, which jointly monitor existing problems, as well as help in dealing with specific legal problems faced by migrant workers from Tajikistan (HRC 2014).

Trade Unions

Migrant Workers' Trade Union (Moscow) publishes a newspaper (in Russian) and holds informational meetings with the new members of the trade union and other migrant workers every last Saturday of the month(HRC 2014).

Private Sector

Although a majority of the migration from Tajikistan is organized primarily through informal means, the role of the private sector, that is, recruiting agencies (commonly referred to as migration agencies in Tajikistan) and employers should not be ignored. In particular, with new destinations, recruiting agencies will grow, as migrants have no networks in the new destination countries. Although the role of the private sector is currently nominal, recruiting agencies can also be a good practice in facilitating higher-skilled migration. Nevertheless, recruiting agencies should be closely monitored to ensure that migrants' rights are protected and they are not charging exorbitant fees. On the other hand, employers in destination countries can be involved in training and recruitment.

---

[9]   Interview with stakeholders.

Proposed Predeparture Orientation Seminar on Safe Migration for Tajik Migrants

A. Basic Propositions

1. **Participants:** The participants of the PDO will be first-time migrants and return migrants who have not taken the course in the last 2 years. However, if any returned migrant (who has taken the course less than 2 years ago) is interested to take the training, they should be provided with the opportunity to participate. The training should be gradually made mandatory for migrants leaving for overseas employment for a year or more.

   In the pilot stage, the seminar can be provided as part of the preemployment skills training under ADB's SEEP project to reach a wider group of potential migrants.

2. Methodology: Methodology of the training should not feature traditional trainer–trainee or student–teacher relationship. The migrants are adults and have their own life experiences. Migrants should be motivated to participate, actively contribute, and change their attitude. Migrants and their families should feel that they have the power to shape their lives, by taking some informed choices.

3. Duration: An optimal course duration for migrants will be 3 days: Days 1 and 2 would be allocated for safe migration awareness, laws and culture at the destination, remittance transfer and use, and other pertinent issues to reap the optimal benefit of migration, and day 3 for family welfare wherein family would also participate. However, the process can also be reduced with the help of digital apps and/or distance learning to 1 day.

At the pilot stage, it is suggested that a day-long course be developed for the migrant workers with 1 hour allocated for a joint session with family members.

It is also highly recommended that if occupational safety procedures and first aid is not covered by skills training, an additional day is allocated for general safety and first aid.

Training time will be 6.5 hours per day, considering tea/coffee, lunch, and prayer break.

4. **Language:** The training will be carried out in Tajik for best possible effectiveness. Where possible, it is highly recommended that in areas where other ethnic languages are prevalent, that language is used as the medium of training. The language of communication, both in the classroom and in printed and electronic materials, should be context and client-specific.

5. **Certification:** A certificate of attendance will be awarded to the trainees on the condition that they have had 100% attendance during the course. The certificate could be a digital part of their registration as well.

6. **When:** The orientation should be organized within 2 weeks of departure so that all the information is firm in their minds. However, tailoring the training program before departure will create difficulties in accommodating varied needs and availability for different categories of migrant workers. The general components of the training should be delivered with supporting documents and digital information on destination countries.

7.   **Supporting materials:** The most important portion of the training topics must be supported by booklets, leaflets, and other printed materials. Information can be supplemented through digital information, further discussed in Recommendations on Digitizing Migration Information and Services.

B.   Training Topics

The focus of safe migration awareness will be for migrants to minimize the risks and achieve successful migration through financial management and protection of family. The information needs of the three stages of migration are discussed briefly in the following:

1. Stage of Predeparture:

- Making arrangements for safe and successful migration.
- Raising awareness on the dangers of irregular migration and human trafficking to discourage migrants into choosing irregular migration when abroad
- Importance of opening a bank account

2. Stage of Travel:

- Preparing for the travel
- Preflight briefing (airport procedure, filling embarkation forms, flight orientation, immigration procedure, etc.); transit and arrival procedures
- Train travel (procedures)
- Entry rights (including what to do if you are on a reentry ban list of the Russian Federation)

3. Stage at the Destination Country:

Registration and Legal Orientation

- Registration in Tajikistan embassies/consulates and its benefits; information should include detailed functions and duties of consular offices, honorary consuls, and representations of migration services.
- Visa and/or work permit/patent procedures and requirements (depending on requirements of

destination countries/regions)[10]

- Registration with the destination country government (importance, requirement, and procedure)
- Tajik migrants have limited knowledge of destination-country-specific migration and labor laws and regulations; awareness on destination country laws relating to migration, work, and stay abroad should be developed; many violations of law are results of lack of knowledge; awareness will encourage migrants to adhere to laws and regulations of the destination country
- Social welfare, medical, and work-related insurance system in the destination countries for migrant workers (how to avail and/or requirements)
- Protecting one's rights and accessing redress mechanisms
- Requirements for bringing the family to destination countries

Cultural Orientation

- General information (geography, language, population, general features, etc.)
- Understanding the culture of the destination country
- Tips on adjustment to the destination country

At the workplace

- Work environment
- Rights and obligations of migrant worker (in case of rights provided by the international and destination country laws)
- Legal orientation on work-related issues and contract
- Labor protection in the destination country
- Irregular status and risks of irregular migration including human trafficking
- Detention and expulsion (for example, this will include tips on how to find out and what to do in case of inclusion in the reentry ban list of the Russian Federation)

Living in the destination country

- Living conditions

---

10   In the case of the Russian Federation, information from each oblast should be provided, as the laws and regulations are different in each oblast.

Box A3.1:   What Does Training Mean?

Training is based on a participatory approach, that is, on the method of participation. What this really means: the entire group actively participates in the process of learning, allowing individuals to share and exchange their knowledge and problems and together search for optimal solutions to their common issues.

Source: IOM Dhaka. 2005. *Facilitators' Guide: English Language Manual for Skilled Migrant Workers,* Annex A, p. 1.

- Health (including sexual and reproductive health, risks and consequences of HIV/AIDS, and communicable diseases and its consequences)
- Transportation

Money management

- Safe banking and remittance services
- Investment opportunities in Tajikistan

4. **Stage of Return and Reintegration:** This will focus on how to optimally utilize the remittance for a sustained and improved impact on livelihood, social status, and esteem. The difficulties of readjustment issues will also be discussed in this section.

5. **Family Well-being:** Information will be provided to migrant workers and their families to make them aware of some issues to discuss with family members, such as remittance management, savings-investment, care and protection of children, health vulnerabilities of family members, reintegration in the family (adjustment), possibilities of exploitation in the family, and change in family structure.

All the important stages of migration will cover "Must Dos and Don'ts" sections, for example, "what to carry and not carry during travel." PDOS will also include a Frequently Asked Questions (FAQs) section.

C.   Methodology of Development and Updating of the Training Program

- **Methodology of Developing the Training Manuals, Booklets, and Other Materials:** Standard training manual for all the subjects need to be developed.

It is strongly recommended that for each topic taught, a resource of accompanying visual aids be developed. Visual aids in the form of wall charts, pictures, flashcards, videos, and so forth greatly enhance the effectiveness of any lesson.

Introduce video materials in some of the sessions, along with lecture and demonstration to dispel the monotony. For example, a video of the different destination countries will give the participants an overview of the country they are going to live and work in.

In addition to training manuals and other materials for the trainers, participants will need a booklet covering important subjects. The booklet should be available in both printed and digital copy. Small booklets or digital apps on destination country languages can also be developed.

- **Updating Training Materials:** In addition to course development, the course will need to be updated regularly. Some of the trainers, based on their performance, can be identified as resources and could serve as a resource pool for continuously upgrading the training.

In addition to regular trainers, NGOs, CSOs, private sector and international organizations, and other agencies should be invited to provide feedback to the training program. The inter-ministerial committee on migration, chaired by MOLME, can take a leading role in this regard.

D.   Structure of the PDOS

- Training Methodology: The training should strongly follow the principles of adult learning. The training methodology should have the following aspects:
  - Participatory approach
  - Trainee centered
  - High use of Information, Education and Communication (IEC) materials

Use of methods, such as pair work, group work, and role play, should be an integral part of the training to maximize active learning and participation of all class members. The trainees must be motivated to take an active part in learning. The focus should be to get all levels (competence of learning) of trainees involved.

The classroom atmosphere must be easy, relaxed, and friendly so that the trainees are not threatened or do not feel shy about making mistakes. It is the trainer's responsibility to help the less competent learners participate equally as the more competent ones. Moreover, the focus should be to encourage the trainees, not to criticize them.

- **Number of Trainees in a Class:** For a trainee-centered methodology to be effectively implemented, a maximum class size of 25 trainees is recommended, which will allow the trainer to provide adequate individual attention.

- **Assessment of Trainees' Performance:** An assessment should be given out at the end of the training; this will enable the trainees to identify their knowledge. The assessment can be written or oral and of a semi-formal nature.

- **Follow-Up Learning:** Some migrants will have considerable time after they complete the course and depart the country. Therefore, trainees should be motivated to continue reading booklets on safe migration and language. Digital apps and/or booklets will also be vital in continuing learning as well as a ready reference guide.

- **Standard Training Room:** It is essential that a suitable learning environment be established for trainees to engage in activities that will best facilitate the practice and acquisition of the targeted skills.

The general criterion for a trainee workspace is to have 0.8 to 1 square meters of individual space excluding trainer and facility space. Moreover, lecture/language classrooms should be large enough to allow trainees to engage in a variety of activities such as group work, pair work, whole class practice, role-play, or whole class "mingling" tasks.

The criteria should be followed in preparing a permanent training room or renting a suitable place for the duration of the training.

- **Training Equipment and Tools:** The assessment proposes the establishment and maintenance of a standard lecture/language classroom with the following items:

  - **A movable whiteboard** (both side usable) and different colored marker pens
  - **Speakers** (the speaker needs to be powerful enough to be heard at the back of a classroom)
  - **Multimedia**
  - **Computer/laptop**
  - **Screen**
  - **Moveable desks** to allow for different room configurations when doing pair work, group work, whole class, or "mingling" activities.
  - **A lockable cupboard** for storage of resources and equipment, in case the training facility is permanent.

Box A3.2:   Who is a Trainer?

One who contributes structure and process and to interactions so groups are able to function effectively and make high-quality decisions. A helper and enabler whose goal is to support others as they achieve exceptional performances.

The person who conducts the training session with a group is called a trainer. Trainers are not teachers in the traditional sense; their role is rather to facilitate the process of learning by the participants, be an intermediary between new knowledge, fresh ideas, and the group. A trainer has certain responsibilities during training—the trainer needs to build a relationship with the group participants. To this end, while working with the group, the trainer should demonstrate in practice her or his belief in the principles of nonviolence and gender equality.

Source: IOM Dhaka. 2005. *Facilitators' Guide: English Language Manual for Skilled Migrant Workers*, Annex A, p. 2.

Box A3.3:   Proposed Monitoring and Evaluation Methods of the Training

The following Monitoring and Evaluation techniques could be adopted for monitoring and evaluating the training program comprehensively:

1. Assessment of Trainers' Performance by Trainee

It is proposed that the trainees are provided with the time log of the course at the beginning of the course and evaluate the performance of trainers by filling in a simple questionnaire in Tajik at the end of the course.

2. Assessment of Trainers' Performance by Stakeholders

An informal monitoring system for trainers is recommended. A joint team of the government and development partners can hold discussions with the trainers and regularly observe classes. It is recommended that any discussions be conducted in an informal friendly manner with the objective of supporting the trainers and allowing them to openly discuss any problems. If trainers do not perform adequately or trainees make legitimate complaints, then new trainers will need to be engaged.

a. Regular Performance Assessment: A designated observer in class can fill up a structured observation tool sheet.

b. Yearly Performance Assessment: It is essential that the trainers are qualified to carry out the new course and familiar with modern teaching techniques. They will need to have an interest in and empathy with the needs of the prospective migrant workers. An individual assessment should be carried out after 1 year of introducing the course and continued every 6 months, and only if they meet the criteria previously mentioned should they be recontracted. In addition, regular health checks need to be performed to ensure that the trainers are physically fit.

3. Assessment of Facilities

Established training centers and rented training rooms both need to be regularly assessed. Trainees can fill in a simple questionnaire and a designated official can evaluate the training rooms according to the standards set in Standard of Training Rooms and Training Equipment and Tools.

4. Assessment and Upgradation of Course Content and Course Timing and Duration

Analysis of the information gathered from the assessments above, feedback from employers and random information collection from returned migrants at the airport could assess the course content and make necessary modifications for the subsequent programs.

Source: International Organization for Migration. 2010. *Practical Guide on Information Provision on Return and Reintegration in Countries of Origin.* Geneva.

- **Childcare support** for women migrants as well as during family orientation should be organized.

- **Flexibility in Course Materials:** The trainees are likely to bring diverse educational and/or skill level, with a wide range of language abilities and varied social background to each class and therefore course materials would need to be flexible and adaptable to meet the needs of different levels and different learning styles.

E.   Selection Criteria and Training of Trainers

- Selection Criteria of Trainers: The following criteria should be maintained for selecting and maintaining instructors:

General:
- *Age:* Younger than 55 years
- *Health:* physically, emotionally, and mentally fit to impart training. Ability to carry out interactive training sessions
- *Education:* university degree, highly recommended to disregard degrees in case the person has experience in dealing with migrant workers and flexibility in adapting to new training methods or has been a migrant worker
- *Language:* knowledge of the destination-country language will be considered as an added skill
- Excellent interpersonal and communication skills

Experience:
- For possible trainers with experience of staying in destination countries, the educational

qualification of university degree and experience of dealing with migrant workers will be relaxed. A migrant worker as a trainer should also be considered as invaluable resource.

– Experience of dealing with migrant workers in information dissemination.
– Experience for conducting predeparture training for migrant workers will be an added qualification.
– Experience in developing or updating training manual/curriculum will be an added qualification.

Test:

A set of procedure of selection needs to be established. Oral and written tests on general information test and suitability test are proposed to be developed for better functioning of the training.

- **Training of Trainers (TOT):** A TOT is compulsory on the materials prepared; the trainers should get a training of trainers' manual with specific guidelines about the methodology and teaching techniques. It is also recommended that regular refresher (at least once a year) courses are held to develop the capacity of the trainers.

The aims of the TOT will be to achieve the following:

- Familiarize trainers with the developed materials
- Explain the aims of the program
- Discuss the methodology and practice techniques to be used in the course
- Familiarize trainers with effective and various uses of the training equipment, that is, computer, multimedia, TV, and other appliances, tools and materials for the training
- Provide information to trainers on relevant aspects of safe migration
- Provide trainers with in-depth training on how to conduct the PDO

The aims of the follow-up/refresher training are the following:

- Discuss and share new teaching techniques
- Allow trainers to share successes of the course and discuss areas for improvement

- Provide an opportunity to make necessary adjustments in the course materials

In addition, training on time management, motivating reluctant trainees, class handling, and so forth needs to be incorporated in the training of trainers.

F. Management of the Training

- **Engaging External Trainers:** Some of the training could be conducted by external trainers. For example, the topic "rights of migrant workers" is better suited to be taken by NGOs since many destination countries have not signed/ratified international laws or do not cover migrants' rights in their domestic law. Therefore, learning about their rights may not be effective if their rights are not respected. Nevertheless, knowledge of their rights should be provided. Experience sharing with returned migrants will also be a positive training tool. In case of unavailability of returned migrants, budget permitting, a video can be developed with experiences of three or four returned migrants, which can be shared in class.

- **Monitoring and Evaluation:** The assessment revealed that the proposed courses will be successfully implemented only with strong monitoring and evaluation and supporting management structure.

Monitoring and evaluation process should take place at two levels: first, the monitoring and evaluation of the training program, and second, monitoring of the trainers. Once the material is developed and is being implemented, there should be constant monitoring and evaluation regarding the effectiveness of both the material and the teaching. The program could be evaluated and reviewed from the following perspectives at the end of each course:

- The course content
- The course timing and duration
- The teaching techniques
- The trainers' performance
- The facilities

A few methods that can be adopted to assess and evaluate the course could be carried out by the trainees and MOLME, which are further discussed in Box A3.3: Proposed Monitoring and Evaluation Methods of the Training..

- **Motivation of Trainers:** A large part of the program's success will depend on the recruitment and retention of trainers of a high standard. In this regard, the remuneration, contractual agreement, and so forth should be considered.
- **Distribution of PDOS:** PDOS can be further strengthened by decentralizing, to improve the popularity, flexibility, and accessibility of their programs. Considering the rate of migration and ensuring maximum coverage, the training will be carried out in the migration centers as a pilot phase and should be expanded to all districts and *jamoats* with high migration rate in the future.

  On the long term, it is strongly recommended that the training distribution area is updated along with the change in the migration trend. In addition, digital apps can complement the PDOS, which is further discussed in Recommendations on Digitizing Migration Information.

- **Information Dissemination on the PDOS:** It is strongly recommended that leaflets be developed to disseminate information about the PDOS. The information may be disseminated by the Migration Centers, Pre-Departure Centers for Migrants, job centers, job fairs, training institutes, ALCs, lyceums, and labor offices at the district centers.

Glossary

Term	Definition
Diaspora	Migrants or descendants of migrants whose identity and sense of belonging, either real or symbolic, have been shaped by their migration experience and background. They maintain links with their homelands, and to each other, based on a shared sense of history, identity, or mutual experiences in the destination country.
	Source: IOM. 2019a. International Migration Law. Working Paper No. 34. *Glossary on Migration.* Geneva. p. 47.
Good practices	A good practice is not only a practice that is good, but a practice that has been proven to work well and produce good results and therefore recommended as a model. It is a successful experience, which has been tested and validated, in the broad sense, which has been repeated and deserves to be shared so that a greater number of people can adopt it.
	Source: FAO. 2003. Good *Practices at FAO: Experience Capitalization for Continuous Learning.* Rome.
Irregular migration	Movement of persons that takes place outside the laws, regulations, or international agreements governing the entry into or exit from the State of origin, transit or destination.
	Source: IOM. 2019a. International Migration Law. Working Paper No. 34. *Glossary on Migration.* Geneva. p. 173.
Migrant	The UN Migration Agency (IOM) defines a migrant as any person who is moving or has moved across an international border or within a State away from his/her habitual place of residence, regardless of (i) the person's legal status; (ii) whether the movement is voluntary or involuntary; (iii) what the causes for the movement are; or (iv) what the length of the stay is.
	Migrant is an umbrella term, not defined under any international law.
Migrant stock (international)	For statistical purposes, the total number of international migrants present in a given country at a particular point in time who have ever changed their country of usual residence.
	Source: Adapted from United Nations Department of Economic and Social Affairs, Toolkit on International Migration. 2012. pp. 2–3. Quoted in IOM. 2019a. International Migration Law. Working Paper No. 34. *Glossary on Migration.* Geneva. p. 134.
Migrant worker	A person engaging in a remunerated activity in a country of which s/he is not a national, excluding asylum seekers and refugees. A *migrant worker* establishes his/her residence in the host country for the duration of his/her work.
	Source: [The International Convention on the Protection of the Rights of All Migrant Workers and Members of Their Families, 1990 has also defined some other migrant workers such as "seafarers," "projectied workers," and "seasonal workers" etc. (Article 2)].
Regular migration	Migration that occurs in compliance with the laws of the country of origin, transit, and destination.
	Source: IOM. 2019a. International Migration Law. Working Paper No. 34. *Glossary on Migration.* Geneva. p. 173.
Remittance	Private international monetary transfers that migrants make, individually or collectively.
	Source: IOM. 2019a. International Migration Law. Working Paper No. 34. Glossary on Migration. Geneva. p. 178.
	It is necessary to distinguish official remittances that are transferred via official bank channels, and are, therefore, recorded in the country's statistics, from unofficial (often referred to as informal) remittances that are sent back via private money courier systems, via friends and relatives, or carried home by the migrants themselves (IOM 2014b).
	Source: IOM. 2014b. *Reference Guide: Labor Attaches of Bangladesh.* Dhaka.

Term	Definition
Reintegration	A process which enables individuals to re-establish the economic, social, and psychosocial relationships needed to maintain life, livelihood, and dignity and inclusion in civic life.
	Note: The various components of reintegration can be described as follows.
	Social reintegration implies the access by a returning migrant to public services and infrastructures in his or her country of origin, including access to health, education, housing, justice, and social protection schemes.
	Psychosocial reintegration is the reinsertion of a returning migrant into personal support networks (friends, relatives, neighbors) and civil society structures (associations, self-help groups, and other organizations). This also includes the re-engagement with the values, mores, way of living, language, moral principles, ideology, and traditions of the country of origin's society.
	Economic reintegration is the process by which a returning migrant re-enters the economic life of his or her country of origin and is able to sustain a livelihood.
	Source: IOM. 2019. International Migration Law. Working Paper No. 34. *Glossary on Migration*. Geneva. p. 174.
Return	In a general sense, the act or process of going back or being taken back to the point of departure. As in the case of migrant workers, between a country of destination or transit and a country of origin.
	Source: IOM. 2019. International Migration Law. Working Paper No. 34. *Glossary on Migration*. Geneva. p. 183.
Return migration	In the context of international migration, the movement of persons returning to their country of origin after having moved away from their place of habitual residence and crossed an international border.
	Source: IOM. 2019. International Migration Law. Working Paper No. 34. *Glossary on Migration*. Geneva. p. 184.
Safe migration	Safe migration does not refer solely to a migrant's safety on the way to and at destination; it also means a migrant's steps to organize migration, safe return of the migrant, reintegration in the family and society, and most importantly long-term stability of achieved success through migration. Therefore, safe migration means successful migration that offers a person a durable foundation to improve his standard of living.
	Note: There is no internationally agreed definition of the term "safe migration."
	Source: IOM Dhaka. 2005b. *Manual on Safe Migration*. Dhaka. p. 21.
Social protection	Social protection is defined as the set of policies and programs designed to reduce poverty and vulnerability by promoting efficient labor markets, diminishing people's exposure to risks, and enhancing their capacity to protect themselves against hazards and interruption/loss of income.
	Note: "Social safety net" and "social security" are sometimes used as an alternative to "social protection." Of the two terms, "social protection" is the most commonly used internationally. The term "social safety net" appears to have a less precise meaning; some people use it to mean the whole set of programs and policies discussed in this strategy; others use it to refer only to welfare programs targeted to the poor. On the other hand, the term "social security" is generally used to refer to the comprehensive mechanisms and coverage in high-income countries and is less applicable to new areas such as community- and area-based schemes.
	Source: ADB. 2003. *Social Protection Strategy*. Manila.
Types of migration from Tajikistan	Some types of (voluntary) migration of Tajiks include (but are not limited to):
	1. **Seasonal labor migrants,** migrants typically leaving Tajikistan for construction, agricultural, or other types of work during the short summer period (March/April to October/November) and returning back home. Could be under a formal or informal (in case of private) contract.
	2. **Temporary labor migrants,** migrate for a year to several years, to work in a state enterprise or a private company or in the informal sector. Temporary labor migrants may be in a settled job in an enterprise for several years. They may also be in an irregular status, meaning they may have entered the destination country legally, but in the course of time have not attained/updated their legal documents and therefore, are not allowed to work in the destination country legally.
	3. **Commercial or shuttle migrants** are traders whose commercial activity is related to regular departures and who return to the country of permanent residence. The purpose is to make a profit. Shuttles exploit inter-regional or international differences in prices and availability of goods (IOM 2003).
	4. **Frontier labor migrants,** who leave the country every day or once a week for paid work.
	5. **Agricultural workers and tenant farmers,** who rent land abroad for cultivation.
	6. **Migration of Muslim clergy.**

Bibliography

Agency of Labor and Employment Tajikistan. http://www.kor.tj/.

ASIA-Plus. 2019a. Putin Signs Law on Ratification of Agreement with Tajikistan on Labor Migrants. 30 December. https://asiaplustj.info/en/news/tajikistan/politics/20191230/putin-signs-law-on-ratification-of-agreement-with-tajikistan-on-labor-migrants.

Asian Development Bank (ADB). 2003. *Social Protection Strategy.* Manila.

———. 2019a. Skills and Employability Enhancement Project (SEEP), Republic of Tajikistan; TA Draft Final Report. Manila.

———. 2019b. Tajikistan 2020–2022. Country Operations Business Plan, Manila, October.

———. 2019c. *Key Indicators for Asia and the Pacific 2019: Tajikistan.* https://data.adb.org/dataset/tajikistan-key-indicators (accessed on 20 January 2020).

———. 2019d. *Key Indicators for Asia and the Pacific 2019: Bangladesh.* https://data.adb.org/dataset/bangladesh-key-indicators (accessed on 20 January 2020).

———. 2019e. *Key Indicators for Asia and the Pacific 2019: Indonesia.* https://data.adb.org/dataset/indonesia-key-indicators (accessed on 20 January 2020).

———. 2019f. *Key Indicators for Asia and the Pacific 2019: Nepal.* https://data.adb.org/dataset/nepal-key-indicators (accessed on 20 January 2020).

———. 2019g. *Key Indicators for Asia and the Pacific 2019: the Philippines.* https://data.adb.org/dataset/philippines-key-indicators (accessed on 20 January 2020).

———. 2019h. *Key Indicators for Asia and the Pacific 2019: the Philippines.* https://data.adb.org/dataset/philippines-key-indicators (accessed on 20 January 2020).

———. 2020a. *Asian Development Outlook 2020: What Drives Innovation in Asia?* Manila.

———. 2020b. The Role of Technology in Assisting Migrants and Facilitating Labor Mobility: A Mapping Exercise. Presentation at ADBI-OECD-ILO Roundtable on Labor Migration in Asia, Future of Labor Migration in Asia, Challenges and Opportunities in the Next Decade. Bangkok, 7 February.

———. *Tajikistan.* https://www.adb.org/countries/tajikistan/main (accessed multiple times during the period from December 2019 to March 2020.

Babaev, Anvar. 2016. *The Migration Situation in Tajikistan: Problems and Solutions.* Central Asian Bureau for Analytical Reporting.

Britannica. *Tajikistan.* https://www.britannica.com/place/Tajikistan/People.

Bureau of Manpower, Employment and Training (BMET). *Overseas Employment in 2019.* http://www.old.bmet.gov. bd/BMET/viewStatReport.action?reportnumber=34 (accessed on 20 January 2020).

———. *Overseas Employment of Female Workers in 2019.* http://www.old.bmet.gov.bd/BMET/viewStatReport. action?reportnumber=29 (accessed on 20 January 2020).

CARAM Asia. 2004. *The Forgotten Spaces, Mobility and HIV/AIDS Vulnerability in Asia.* Regional Generic Manual. Kuala Lumpur.

Central Intelligence Agency. Central Asia: Tajikistan—The World Factbook. https://www.cia.gov/library/ publications/the-world-factbook/geos/print_ti.html.

Civil Society Contact Group Tajikistan. 2016. *Changing Patterns of Labor Migration in Tajikistan.* International Alert. March. https://www.international-alert.org/sites/default/files/Tajikistan_LaborMigrationPatterns_EN_2016.pdf.

Department of International Development. 2015. *The Impact of the 2014–15 Russian Economic Crisis on Migrants from Tajikistan and Kyrgyzstan.* Dushanbe.

The Diplomat. 2019. Why Is Kazakhstan a Growing Destination for Central Asian Migrant Workers? 13 June. https://thediplomat.com/2019/06/why-is-kazakhstan-a-growing-destination-for-central-asian-migrant-workers/.

———. 2020. Russia Ratifies Agreement With Tajikistan on Labor Migrants. 3 January. https://thediplomat. com/2020/01/russia-ratifies-agreement-with-tajikistan-on-labor-migrants/.

EU Neighbours. 2016. Moldova: PARE 1+1—Encouraging Migrants to Return Home. 13 October. https://www. euneighbours.eu/en/east/eu-in-action/stories/moldova-pare-11-encouraging-migrants-return-home.

Eurasianet. 2018. Tajikistan: Is Islamic Banking the Future? 24 January. https://eurasianet.org/tajikistan-is-islamic-banking-the-future.

European Training Foundation. 2010. *Migration Survey: Migration and Skills in Tajikistan.* Turin, Italy.

European University Institute. 2014. Regional Migration Report: Russia and Central Asia. Fiesole, Italy.

Food and Agriculture Organization of the United Nations (FAO). 2003. *Good Practices at FAO: Experience Capitalization for Continuous Learning.* Rome.

FAO. 2019. Developing Capacity for Strengthening Food Security and Nutrition. 24 January. http://www.fao.org/ in-action/fsn-caucasus-asia/news/news-detail/en/c/1178555/.

Garip, Filiz, and Asad L. Asad. 2015. Migrant Networks. Emerging Trends in the Social and Behavioral Sciences: An Interdisciplinary, Searchable, and Linkable Resource: 1–13. doi: 10.1002/9781118900772.etrds0220

Global Knowledge Partnership on Migration and Development (KNOMAD). 2020. *COVID-19 Crisis: Through a Migration Lens.* Migration and Development Brief 32, Washington, DC.

Government of Nepal. 2016. Labor Migration for Employment—A Status Report for Nepal: 2014/2015. Kathmandu.

Government of Tajikistan. 1991. Law of the Republic of Tajikistan on Migration, No. 881. Dushanbe.

———. 2016. *National Development Strategy of the Republic of Tajikistan for the Period up to 2030.* Dushanbe.

Human Rights Center (HRC). 2014. *Legal Protection of Migrant Workers from Tajikistan in the Russian Federation.* Dushanbe.

International Federation for Human Rights and Anti-Discrimination Center «Memorial» (FIDH/ADC). 2014. *From Tajikistan to Russia: Vulnerability and Abuse of Migrant Workers and Their Families.* Paris.

International Labour Organization (ILO). 2003. *The International Convention on the Protection of the Rights of All Migrant Workers and Members of Their Families, 1990.* Geneva.

———. 2010a. *Migrant Remittances to Tajikistan: The Potential for Savings, Economic Investment and Existing Financial Products to Attract Remittances.* Moscow.

———. 2010b. *Migration and Development in Tajikistan—Emigration, Return and Diaspora.* Moscow.

———. 2014. *Assessment of the Existing Services for Skilled Migrant Workers in the Philippines.* Manila.

———. 2015. *Manual on General Migrant.* Bangladesh.

———. 2018. *Skills for Migration and Employment.* Policy Brief. Skills for Employment. Geneva.

———. 2020. Digitization and Future of Migration. Presentation at ADBI-OECD-ILO Roundtable on Labor Migration in Asia, Future of Labor Migration in Asia, Challenges and Opportunities in the Next Decade. Bangkok, 7 February.

———. www.ilo.org.

International Monetary Fund (IMF). 2020. *World Economic Outlook.* Chapter 1, Washington, DC, April.

International Organization for Migration (IOM). No date. Community Stabilization and Emergencies. http://www.iom.tj/index.php/en/activities/community-stabilization (accessed on 24 January 2020).

———. No date. Best Practices: IOM's Migrant Training / Pre-Departure Orientation Programs. https://www.iom.int/jahia/webdav/shared/shared/mainsite/activities/facilitating/Best-Practices-Migrant-Training.pdf.

———. 2003. *Labor Migration from Tajikistan.* Dushanbe.

———. 2005a. *Labor Migration in Asia: Protection of Migrant Workers, Support Services and Enhancing Development Benefits.* Geneva.

———. 2005b. *Manual on Safe Migration.* Bangladesh.

———. 2006. *English Language Manual for Skilled Migrant Workers.* Dhaka.

———. 2010a. *Practical Guide on Information Provision on Return and Reintegration in Countries of Origin.* Geneva.

———. 2010b. *Labor Migration from Indonesia: An Overview of Indonesian Migration to Selected Destinations in Asia and the Middle East.* Jakarta.

———. 2012. Strengthening Pre-departure Orientation Programs in Indonesia, Nepal and the Philippines. Issue in Brief. Issue No. 5. Bangkok.

———. 2014a. *Tajik Migrants with Re-entry Bans to the Russian Federation.* Dushanbe.

———. 2014b. *Reference Guide: Labor Attaches of Bangladesh.* Dhaka.

———. 2015. *Diaspora—Partner in the Development of Tajikistan.* Dushanbe.

———. 2017a. *Migrants' Right to Health in Central Asia: Challenges and Opportunities.* Bishkek.

———. 2017b. *Migrant Vulnerabilities and Integration Needs in Central Asia: Assessing Migrants' and Community Needs and Managing Risks.* Astana.

———. 2018a. *Summary Report: Fragile Power of Migration: The Needs and Rights of Women and Girls from Tajikistan and Kyrgyzstan Who Are Affected by Migration.* Dushanbe.

———. 2018b. *Return and Reintegration: Key Highlights.* Geneva.

———. 2018c. *A Framework for Assisted Voluntary Return and Reintegration.* Geneva.

———. 2018d. *The Mapping and Scoping of Services for The Migrant Workers of Bangladesh at Various Stages of Labor Migration Cycle.* Bangladesh.

———. 2019a. Glossary on Migration. International Migration Law. Working Paper No. 34. Geneva.

———. 2019b. *World Migration Report 2020.* Geneva.

———. 2019c. *External Youth Migration in the Countries of Central Asia: Risk Analysis and Minimization of Negative Consequences.* Kazakhstan.

———. *Tajikistan.* https://www.iom.int/countries/tajikistan.

IOM Tajikistan. Labor Migration. http://www.iom.tj/index.php/en/activities/labor-migration

Japan International Cooperation Agency (JICA). 2018. *Household Survey: Migration, Living Conditions and Skills: Panel Study—Tajikistan, 2018.* Tokyo.

———. 2019. *Household Survey: Migration, Living Conditions and Skills: Panel Study—Tajikistan, 2019.* Tokyo.

———. 2020. IOM Global Strategic Preparedness and Response Plan: Coronavirus Disease 2019 (February–December 2020) 15 April.

Masud Ali, A. K. 2005. Pre-Departure Orientation Program: Study of Good Practices in Asia—A Comparative Study of Bangladesh, the Philippines and Sri Lanka. In *Labour Migration in Asia: Protection of Migrant Workers, Support Services and Enhancing Development Benefits.* Geneva: International Organization for Migration.

Migration Policy Institute (MPI). 2006. Tajikistan: From Refugee Sender to Labor Exporter. Migration Information Source. 1 July. https://www.migrationpolicy.org/article/tajikistan-refugee-sender-labor-exporter.

———. 2013. The Growing Linkages Between Migration and Microfinance. Migration Information Source. 13 June. https://www.migrationpolicy.org/article/growing-linkages-between-migration-and-microfinance.

———. 2019. Dependent on Remittances, Tajikistan's Long-Term Prospects for Economic Growth and Poverty Reduction Remain Dim. Migration Information Source. 14 November. https://www.migrationpolicy.org/article/dependent-remittances-tajikistan-prospects-dim-economic-growth.

Ministry of Labor and Employment, Government of Nepal. 2018. *Labor Migration for Employment: A Status Report for Nepal – 2015-16 – 2016-17.* https://asiafoundation.org/wp-content/uploads/2018/05/Nepal-Labor-Migration-status-report-2015-16-to-2016-17.pdf (accessed on 20 January 2020).

Ministry of Labor, Migration and Employment of the Population of the Republic of Tajikistan. http://mehnat.tj/mehnat/en/main/.

MOU between MOLME and ADB for TA 9639-TAJ: The Skills and Employability Enhancement Project (SEEP). 2019. TRTA Final Review/Grant Fact Finding Mission. 4–19 November.

The National Board for the Placement and Protection of Indonesian Overseas Workers (BNP2TKI). 2019. Presentation at Strengthening the Collection and Use of International Migration Data in The Context of the 2030 Agenda for Sustainable Development. Bangkok, 5–8 February. https://www.unescap.org/sites/default/files/3%20Session%207%20Country%20presentation%20Indonesia.pdf (accessed on 20 January 2020).

Open Working Group on Labor Migration & Recruitment. No date. *Policy Brief 3. Government-to-Government Recruitment Benefits & Drawbacks.*

Organization for Security and Co-operation in Europe (OSCE), International Organization for Migration (IOM), and International Labour Organization (ILO). 2006. *Handbook on Establishing Effective Labour Migration Policies in Countries of Origin and Destination.* Helsinki.

Overseas Workers Welfare Administration (OWWA). *Reintegration Program.* https://www.owwa.gov.ph/index.php/programs-services/reintegration (accessed on 19 February 2020).

Philippine Statistics Authority. *2018 Survey on Overseas Filipinos.* Table 1.1: Distribution of Overseas Filipino Workers 2018. https://psa.gov.ph/statistics/survey/labor-and-employment/survey-overseas-filipinos/table (accessed on 20 January 2020).

PwC. Worldwide Tax Summaries Online. *Tajikistan—Individual and Other Taxes.* http://taxsummaries.pwc.com/ID/Tajikistan-Individual-Other-taxes.

Quddusov, Jamshed. 2011. Evaluation of Services Provided to Labor Migrants by Dushanbe Pre-Departure Service Center (draft). Unpublished.

Sri Lanka Bureau of Foreign Employment (SLBFE). *Annual Statistical Report of Foreign Employment 2017.* http://www.slbfe.lk/file.php?FID=487 (accessed on 20 January 2020).

Swiss Agency for Development and Cooperation (SDC). 2018. *Briefing Note. Technology, Migration and the 2030 Agenda for Sustainable Development.* Bern.

United Nations Development Programme (UNDP). 2019a. Republic of Moldova Engages Migrants in Local Development and Creates Reintegration Services for Returning Migrants. 31 July. https://www.md.undp.org/content/moldova/en/home/presscenter/pressreleases/2019/republica-moldova-implic-migranii-in-dezvoltarea-economic-local-.html.

———. 2019b. Moldova Selects Partner Communities and Hometown Associations to Contribute to Local Development. Press Release. 26 August. https://moldova.un.org/en/14633-undp-moldova-selects-partner-communities-and-hometown-associations-contribute-local.

United Nations Economic Commission for Europe. 2018. *Statistics on International Migration in Russia: the Current Situation.* Conference of European Statisticians. Work Session on Migration Statistics. Working Paper 11, Geneva, 24–26 October.

United Nations High Commissioner for Refugees (UNHCR). 2017. *The 10-Point Plan.* Geneva.

United Nations Joint Migration and Development Initiative (JMDI). 2011. *Migration for Development: a Bottom-Up Approach—A Handbook for Practitioners and Policymakers.* Brussels.

United Nations. *Tajikistan.* https://esa.un.org/miggmgprofiles/indicators/files/Tajikistan.pdf.

———. https://www.un.org/en/sections/issues-depth/migration/index.html.

UN News. Migrants Among Most Vulnerable, as IOM Ramps up Coronavirus Response Worldwide. 15 April. https://news.un.org/en/story/2020/04/1061842?fbclid=IwAR3qzPMLOeI4AiioRocd-iATxeWy9_1Fg-iy47GSvwItY-ozMMY0bp4iAsE (accessed on 20 April 2020).

University of Sussex. 2007. *Migration and Poverty Reduction in Tajikistan.* Development Research Centre on Migration, Globalisation and Poverty, Working Paper C11, Brighton.

US Department of State. 2019. *2019 Trafficking in Persons Report: Russia.* Washington, DC. https://www.state.gov/reports/2019-trafficking-in-persons-report-2/russia/.

Wikipedia. *Tajikistan.* https://en.wikipedia.org/wiki/Tajikistan.

World Bank. *Migration and Remittances Data; Annual Remittances Data.* https://www.worldbank.org/en/topic/migrationremittancesdiasporaissues/brief/migration-remittances-data (accessed on 20 January 2020).

———. 2018. *Moving for Prosperity: Global Migration and Labor Markets.* Policy Research Report. Washington, DC.

———. 2020. World Bank Predicts Sharpest Decline of Remittances in Recent History. Press Release. 22 April. https://www.worldbank.org/en/news/press-release/2020/04/22/world-bank-predicts-sharpest-decline-of-remittances-in-recent-history.

World Bank Group. 2019. *Migration and Remittances: Recent Development and Outlooks.* Migration and Development Brief 31, Washington, DC.

www.ingramcontent.com/pod-product-compliance
Lightning Source LLC
Chambersburg PA
CBHW051657210326
41518CB00026B/2613